KAREN HOBBS

Swept Away

THE VANISHING ART OF BROOM MAKING

Schiffer Publishing Ltd
4880 Lower Valley Road • Atglen, PA 19310

Library of Congress Control Number: 2017935743

Cover design by Brenda McCallum
Zachary Alan Photography—Pattern Section
Various Artists—Gallery
Karen Hobbs—Miscellaneous

Type set in Amplitude, Lobster & Carioca

ISBN: 978-0-7643-5445-8
Printed in China
5 4 3 2

MIX
Paper | Supporting responsible forestry
FSC® C104723

Published by Schiffer Publishing, Ltd.
4880 Lower Valley Road
Atglen, PA 19310
Phone: (610) 593-1777; Fax: (610) 593-2002
E-mail: Info@schifferbooks.com
Web: www.schifferbooks.com

Contents

Introduction

There are many stories about how brooms got their start in the United States. It seems everyone agrees Benjamin Franklin is responsible for bringing brooms to the Americas. One of my favorite stories was told to me by Ray LeBlanc of PelRay International: When the Egyptian pharaohs needed to clean the floors of their palaces from the dust and sands of the desert, they asked their agronomists to develop a straw or fiber that could be used to clean and trap dust. What they invented was broomcorn. The hard, outer shell of the fiber combined with the soft, pithy interior and the flexibility of the fiber allowed the hard exterior to splinter continuously, and the tiny splinters catch dust and are constantly renewed.

When Ben Franklin was ambassador to France, he made a trip to Egypt. While he was there he saw some of these "broomcorn" brooms and was fascinated by the way the fibers worked trapping dust. One of the brooms still had some seed on the fiber and Ben plucked off the seeds and kept them.

When Ben got back to the United States, he planted the seeds and harvested the first broomcorn ever grown in the US and/or North America. He made some brooms for his personal use and broomcorn has been growing in North America ever since.

Sam Moyer of New Jersey told me about an excerpt from "The Papers of Benjamin Franklin" explaining the role he played in introducing broomcorn to America. I obtained a copy of a letter Ben wrote to his sister, Jane Mecom, in Philadelphia, on February 21, 1757:

> I enclose you some whisk seed; it is a kind of corn, good for creatures; it must be planted in hills, like Indian corn. The tops make the best thatch in the world; and of the same are made the whisks you use for velvet. Pray try if it will grow with you. I brought it from Virginia. Give some to Mr. Cooper, some to Mr. Bowdoin.

On March 24, 1757, he wrote to American statesman Samuel Ward:

> I enclose you some of the grain called Whisk Corn, or Broom Corn. It must be planted in Hills like Indian Corn, three or four grains in a hill. It looks like Indian Corn when growing, till the Top comes out, of which they make the Whisk Brushes for Velvet, and excellent Brooms. The Grain is good for Bread, and for Fowls, Horses, &c. being a kind of Millet, and of great increase. The Stalks &c. make excellent Thatch. It grows ten foot high, and I believe must have a little more room than you commonly give your Indian Corn; but plant it at the same time. When tis ripe, gather it; you may strip the Seed off by Hand, from the Whisk, or your Fowls will pick it off. Give my dear Friend Katy enough of the tops to make a whisk for her Mantelet. . . .[1]

Put yourself in the place of the early American housewife for a moment: there you are with a house full of dirt—no broom, no vacuum cleaner, no carpet sweeper, and no other handy helper. All you have is a bundle of twigs tied to a handle. About all you can do is push the dirt around your hearth and floors with this gadget called a "besom"(*bee'-some*). It leaves interesting tracks in the dirt, but does not do much else. But wait! Here comes good old Ben Franklin to the rescue!

One day when he was not busy flying kites or speaking sage sayings, Ben Franklin sowed the seeds for a strange plant he had brought back from Egypt, or Hungary, or wherever his travels had taken him. This plant was called broomcorn, and with it he earned the undying gratitude of millions upon millions of Americans who could burn their besoms and pick up their handy-dandy, honest-to-goodness brooms!

Since the first broomcorn broom Franklin introduced in 1790, there have been many other brooms and brushes made, but the king of them all is still Ben's broomcorn broom. No one has ever figured out how to improve it, since it is one of the most efficient and economical cleaning tools we have. You can feel the reason for this continued success by running your fingers up the broom stalks. The prickly little "hairs" you feel catch and hold dirt and dust. Synthetic broom fibers do not have these built-in catchers, which is why they are not as efficient at cleaning. It is really amazing how much we owe to the inventive genius of Ben Franklin.

CHAPTER ONE

History

For more than a century, a good broom was one of an American housewife's most prized possessions. No other fiber equals broomcorn for picking up dust and sweeping. Broomcorn is a natural product grown specifically for brooms. It is a unique fiber to which no other material can compare. Since 1950, vacuums have picked up fifty percent of the nation's broom market. Broomcorn still fights the battle of cleanliness in homes daily. It has quite a "pedigree," probably originating in Africa, where its older relative, kafir, is believed to be native. Broomcorn is a tall, cultivated plant derived from a variety of sorghum, which is the family name for a kind of tropical plant. By definition, a broom is a cleaning tool consisting of still fibers attached to, and roughly parallel to, a cylindrical handle—a broomstick. A broom maker is a person that creates broomsticks. Up until the early twentieth century, most broomsticks were created by individual broom makers. For more than 250 years, broom makers have not found a better material for brooms than broomcorn. Broomcorn (*Sorghum vulgare var. technicum*) is a type of sorghum used for making all types of brooms: kitchen, hearth, car, cobweb, and whisk. It is sometimes called millet or guinea corn. It differs from other sorghums in that it produces heads with fibrous seed branches as much as thirty-six inches long. *Encyclopedia Britannica* defines broomcorn as a variety of upright grass of the species *Sorghum vulgare* (or *S. bicolor variety technicum*) belonging to the family *Gramineae* (sometimes *Poaceae*) that is cultivated for their stiff stems. Broomcorn is also used to make decorative items, such as wreaths, floral arrangements, and baskets.

The broomcorn plant was first described in Italy in the late 1500s. Benjamin Franklin is credited with introducing broomcorn to the United States in the early 1700s. One story goes that after a friend had given him a broom as a gift to clean his hats he found a few seeds on the broom and planted them. The seeds grew broomcorn, which he tied together and made a broom. Broomcorn was produced in Texas, Colorado, Illinois, New Mexico, Iowa, Oklahoma, and Kansas. Today some broomcorn is grown in Illinois. Arcola, Illinois, is still known to many as the "Broomcorn Capital of the World." The majority of broomcorn is imported from Mexico due to land and labor costs. Broomcorn is also imported from Hungary, China, Indonesia, and Paraguay.

Brooms have been used for hundreds of years to sweep caves, cabins, and castles. Tree branches and brush were often used to sweep floors and clean ashes from fireplaces. The wing from a turkey was also used to clean fireplaces, thus today we make the "turkey wing whisk broom." Willow and birch besoms (*besom* is the Germanic term for broom) were produced and sold in Europe. Heather brooms were made in England, Scotland, and Wales. Initially, broomcorn was grown only as a garden crop for use in the home. By 1834, commercial broomcorn production had started. Illinois was the leading producer in 1860, but production in that state virtually ceased in 1967.

US demand for broomcorn has declined with the rise in sales of synthetic brooms. There are still a number of artisan craftsmen who pride themselves in making quality brooms by hand. Broomsquires—people who make their living as broom makers—make round and flat brooms. Round brooms are considered European, since it was first made in Europe before the New World. When the colonies were settled, women would sew brooms below the handle. This is where they got the name "colonial broom." At first, men would not allow women to sew brooms because it looked worldly and their Puritan religion would not allow it. After all, they came to the New World so they could practice their religion. Folklore has it that women explained to the men that by sewing the broom below the handle it made sweeping faster and the broom last longer, so they had more time to worship God. The women won, and that is how the colonial broom came into being. The Shakers are responsible for flattening the broom, like the kitchen broom we know today. Shakers in New England and slaves in the South simultaneously made the change, sewing their brooms flat for better coverage when sweeping.

In times of slavery in the US, enslaved African couples were denied all rights, including the right to be formally married and live together. Because they could not legally marry, they created their own rituals to honor their unions. To make a public declaration of their love and commitment, a man and woman would literally jump over a broom into matrimony. The jumping of the broom is a symbol of sweeping away the old and welcoming the new, or a symbol of a new beginning. Many couples today are choosing to include this ceremony in their own weddings. It is a ceremony dating back to the 1600s, derived from Africa. The straws of the broom represent family and the handle represents the Almighty.[1]

The brooms of yesteryear were crude and inefficient. One was made by tying twigs together to a stick. Another was made by splitting a hickory stick about four feet long from the end to within a few inches of the other end, then wetting and bending the small splinters down and tying them in the form of a bundle.[2]

In the twenty-first century, you will find manufactured brooms out of broomcorn with the middle layer utilizing swamp grass or bear grass. During WWI, swamp grass was substituted for the insides of brooms. After WWI, broom prices fell and the demand for swamp grass fiber disappeared. This cuts down on the amount of natural broomcorn used for each broom, thus cutting down on cost. Manufacturers will also turn to this method when there has been a drought in Mexico and broomcorn is in short supply.

Harve Pelton sent Mr. Kerr to Buenos Aires, Argentina, to buy broomcorn during the period of high prices (1910). *Courtesy of Bart Pelton*

Allen Andrew Simonson (left, 1918) was Bart Pelton's great-grandfather. He was sent to Florida to buy, cut, and bale "swamp grass"for selling to broom factories as a low price substitute fiber for broom insides. *Courtesy of Bart Pelton*

Unloading broomcorn at the shipyard, 1910. *Courtesy of Bart Pelton*

Bear grass today. *Courtesy of Karen Hobbs*

CHAPTER TWO

Growing Broomcorn

Named for its large, broom-like, fibrous tassel head, broomcorn is grown much like oats or barley. It is a warm, dry climate crop, usually planted between May 1 and June 15. Seeds range from two to four pounds per acre. The seeds are small and off-white in color, and produce large heads of grain that are collected specifically to make brooms. Broomcorn is a labor intensive crop harvested by hand. It can be grown in sandy soils and rich bottomlands.

Seed bed preparation involves plowing, disking, and narrowing.[1] Broomcorn is planted in rows and cultivated like ordinary field corn. It is a tall plant that resembles sweet corn. The standard varieties grow ten to fifteen feet high and are used mainly for carpet brooms. The dwarf varieties of broomcorn"mostly grown today"reach two to six feet. These plants resemble corn, and the seed clusters of broomcorn grow at the top of the stem, like the tassels of corn.[2] It takes forty to fifty plants to make a broom. Each plant produces a stalk that branches out from twenty to forty fibers. The average crop produces 20 25,000 tons. It takes approximately ninety days to mature a crop; it will mature on less moisture than Indian corn and will stand lots of wet weather if not too late in its growth. It is said the "best brush" is produced when summers are warm and soil is moist and fertile. Annual rainfall of fifteen to thirty-two inches is adequate.

In the mid-1800s, Illinois was a prime area for growing broomcorn because of its climate and fertile soil. Through World War II, Arcola, Illinois, claimed the heaviest concentration of broomcorn farms on earth. Patrick H. Monahan became the first broomcorn broker in Illinois in 1869, and he paved the way to making Arcola known as the Broomcorn Capital of the World. Around 1910, Lindsay, Oklahoma, was known as the Broomcorn Capital of the United States for many years. The broomcorn grown around Lindsay was considered higher quality than any other growing districts. Local farmers no longer grow broomcorn. Because of high labor costs for harvesting by migrant workers, Arcola farmers switched to more profitable crops. In Mexico, longer harvesting seasons lead to two yearly crops and plentiful, inexpensive labor—the crop is more economically raised.

In 2014, Arcola held their forty-fourth annual Broom Corn Festival. During this three-day event they had a 10K and a 5K race, a Jaycees' kiddie tractor pull, a national broom sweeping contest, the annual handmade broom contest, live entertainment, a parade with the famous Lawn Rangers, and lots of vendors, food, and fun for the entire family. The world famous Lawn Rangers became the first ever precision broom and lawn mower drill team to march in the presidential inaugural parade on January 20, 2009. They have two trademark maneuvers: "Walk the Dog" and "Cross and Toss." My husband and I were invited by Pat Monahan to participate in the parade. What an exciting day!

In the broomcorn tent you will find the famous handmade broom competition on display and the Humboldt Broom Factory booth, with owner Louie Turner and his daughter, Jodie, selling beautiful brooms. The reproduction of the Broomcorn Palace of 1898 is by the entrance. According to Pat Monahan, in 1898, the original Broomcorn Palace was in the middle of Main Street, where horse-drawn vehicles could pass through the opening in the lower level of the palace. It was completely covered and thatched with broomcorn. Mr. Monahan says no one has ever duplicated the original palace, but it is tradition to have one at every festival.

Monahan Partners broomcorn plot, Arcola, Illinois, 2013. *Courtesy of Karen Hobbs*

Multi-colored broomcorn seeds. *Courtesy of Karen Hobbs*

The Broomcorn Palace today at the Arcola Broomcorn Festival, 2013. *Courtesy of Karen Hobbs*

The Broomcorn Palace 1898, on display at the Arcola Broomcorn Festival, 2013. *Courtesy of Karen Hobbs*

Mural in Arcola, Illinois. *Courtesy of Karen Hobbs*

The Lawn Rangers, a precision broom and lawn mower drill team. *Courtesy of the World Famous Lawn Rangers*

CHAPTER THREE

Harvesting Broomcorn

Broomcorn will grow five to eight feet tall, and good corn has fifty to sixty fibers. Harvesting the crop and preparing it for a broom maker requires a great deal of hand labor. If harvested before mature more broomcorn fiber is present and more fiber is not brittle. Because the broomcorn is sometimes eight feet tall it must be brought down to the worker's height, so the process of tabling must be done. First, a man walks backward between two rows and breaks over the stalks crisscross to form what is known as a "table." The broomcorn is broken at the first knuckle. Warm temperatures in the day and cool nights make the fibers kink at the knuckle. These stalks are less desirable to the broom makers and are used on the inner layer of brooms. Cutting the table is a very hard and dangerous task using a sharp knife. The worker grasps the brush in one hand, pulls the stem against the blade of the knife, and exerts an outward pull at the same time. Each brush is cut off just below the crown and piled in handfuls on this table. These are hauled to a machine with whirling, spiked cylinders which knock off the seed. When growing your own, you can remove seeds with a long-toothed curry comb or make a comb out of a board by sawing teeth into one end of it. You could also thresh it. The brush is then spread on racks in a drying shed (rick curing), where after curing for two or three weeks, it is compressed into bales weighing 300 to 450 pounds. All this must be done carefully to yield good untangled fiber for use in brooms. In Mexico broomcorn is dried outside. After it is piled up it is covered to prevent bleaching by the sun.[1] Harvesting is all accomplished by hand. Workers can harvest 500—1,000 kilos a day. This labor was once done by large groups of migrating laborers known as "canaries" or "johnnies." Harvesting usually begins in September.

Harvested broomcorn is placed on racks, then in sheds to dry. *Courtesy of Bart Pelton*

Broom making as a low-tech and agricultural industry was one of the first in the United States to move out of the country into a rapidly developing global economy. Broomcorn harvesting did not mechanize as did harvesting of other crops; the process has not essentially changed from the nineteenth century to today. Except for the substitution of a tractor for a horse, the mechanization revolution in agriculture passed broomcorn by; all harvesting is still being done by hand because of the delicate nature of the tassels. Thus, when American agriculture mechanized in the mid-twentieth century and agricultural hand labor began to cost relatively more than machinery, most broomcorn production ended in the United States.

According to Dr. Sam Moyer of Mount Laurel, New Jersey, broomcorn is one of the easiest domestic plants to grow. It takes him over seventy hours to prepare 300 pounds of seed brush from tabling it in the field to seeding and sorting it for use in brooms. In 1983, Dr. Moyer and Dr. Henry Hadley of the University of Illinois developed a shorter, machine harvestable hybrid broomcorn that is also easier to harvest by knife or reaper. Crosses were made from heirloom varieties to produce desirable genetic traits, including short plants. He says the brush has nearly all the colors of the rainbow. Seed is available from Dr. Moyer.[2]

CHAPTER FOUR

Sorting Broomcorn

Sorting broomcorn in the classroom. *Courtesy of Karen Hobbs*

Bales of hurl in the warehouse at PelRay. *Courtesy of Karen Hobbs*

At the factory, broomcorn is sorted according to length, color (green is preferred), fiber quality, inside hurl, and center stims (which are pulled out). While sorting, hurl is placed in barrels called "bumping machines" to get fibers even for baling. The selector machine separates broomcorn into various lengths for correlating bens. It is important for workers to keep a constant stream of broomcorn going through to make the process more efficient. As it goes through the selector machine the hurl is cut off at the knuckle. There are four lengths: regular—the inside of the broomcorn; hurl, which takes up to ten to fifteen percent of the longest fibers; warehouse; and crook neck.

The Mohawk Valley region of New York was found to raise a much better brush than Massachusetts, so the crop migrated there, and soon the manufacturing of brushes was started there as well and flourished for years. Here the Niskayuna Shakers went into raising the brush and making it into brooms. Here also brooms changed their shapes. Rougher corn was put on the inside and more of it put on two sides of the handle opposite each other, and the result was then flattened by a press to hold it in shape. This added to the broom's present streamlined appearance and to its sales volume. It was here the first machines were used to wind wire around the handle and over the layers of fiber, enabling a man to make several times the number of brooms he could tie by hand. Then migrating mankind carried the seed and idea to Ohio and Tennessee. There are seven distinct varieties of broomcorn: Evergreen, Black Spanish, California Golden, Scarborough, Black Spanish Dwarf, Japanese Dwarf, and White Italian (was grown extensively in Illinois).

CHAPTER FIVE

Dying Broomcorn

Dying broomcorn adds a decorative touch to a utilitarian broom. It is a labor intensive process that expands over many hours and days. To dye broomcorn, one must have optimum weather for drying after the dying is complete. Due to the time it takes for the dye to soak into broomcorn it takes a few days for it to dry. It may feel dry to the touch and not be dry deep in the core. Natural dyes are more inconsistent when it comes to dying broomcorn; they do not penetrate the waxy outer layer of the broomcorn. Chemical dyes are used for a more consistent color penetration, and are used with a presoak of a surfactant (some say Dawn dish soap works, or simply soaking in scalding hot water). The surfactant breaks down the waxy outer layer of the broomcorn and allows chemical dyes to penetrate with a more consistent color transformation. These chemical dyes are more colorfast and will not fade over time compared to natural dyes.

Natural hurl baled. *Courtesy of Karen Hobbs*

Dyed hurl. *Courtesy of Karen Hobbs*

CHAPTER SIX

The Legacy of Broomcorn

Broom and Broom Corn News, first issue. *Courtesy of BBM, Photo by Karen Hobbs*

Broom, Brush & Mop Centennial 1912–2012 issue. *Courtesy of BBM, Photo by Karen Hobbs*

The first installment of *Broom and Broom Corn News* was issued February 27, 1912. The publication was started in Arcola, Illinois, by brothers Frank F. and W. L. "Roy" Collins. They served not only as the publication's owners, but also its editors and publishers. For many years prior to 1912, the Collins brothers had devoted a page or more of each issue of their *Arcola Record-Herald* to news about broomcorn and allied industries. The newspaper's "Broom Corn Corner" was a regular department of the *Record-Herald*. Frank Collins would remain owner of *Broom and Broom Corn News* until 1941.

Broom and Broom Corn News started as a weekly publication with a subscription of $1 per year in the United States and $1.50 a year for those readers in foreign countries.

Included in the first issue was a detailed statement listing the number of counties, farms, acres, and pounds of broom corn by state grown in 1909, according to the 1910 census. For example, it showed there were 1,854 farms in sixty-nine Illinois counties that grew broomcorn. This involved 38,452 acres, yielding 19,309,425 pounds with a total value of $1,457,172. Of the forty-eight states in 1909, all but Florida, Idaho, Maine, Montana, Nevada, New Hampshire, Oregon, Rhode Island, Vermont, and Wyoming grew some amount of broomcorn. Oklahoma led the nation in most categories with 10,151 farms,

216,350 acres, 42,741,725 pounds, and a total broom corn value of $2,559,235.

The July 15, 1913, issue reported the governor of Kansas received an appeal from farmers in the western part of the state, asking him to invoke an old, outdated law to aid in the fight against grasshoppers. The article stated that the old law was long unused and was first enacted just after the great grasshopper invasions in Kansas during 1873. The law provided that, "Every able-bodied man, woman and child between the ages of 12 and 60 years be called upon to fight grasshoppers." The article added that farmers had reported thousands of dollars of losses to crops from grasshoppers. The article did not state just how the grasshoppers were to be eliminated.

The January 30, 1917, issue of *Broom and Broom Corn News* reported that 504 (rail) cars of broomcorn valued at $1,149,000 were shipped from Lindsay, Oklahoma, in 1916. It also reported this area had seen an increase in oil production.

The July 24, 1917, issue reported on a labor shortage, as the draft for World War I was taking place. The article stated, "Some young manufacturers and broom corn dealers and buyers were included in the draft and there will have to be some changes to certain businesses." There continued to be a shortage of workers for broomcorn fields during WWI and through the 1930s and 1940s.

Through the 1960s and 1970s, the *Broom and Broom Corn News* remained essentially the same as during the publication's previous decades. The faithful reader would notice more and more photos included, and the use of color in advertisements.

March 16, 1974, the news was centered on what was happening in Mexico, which was becoming a common topic. "U.S. buyers have been devoting special attention to the Mexican market the past few weeks as the first of the 1974 crop is being harvested in the Apatzingán area. The November 26, 1977, issue announced the purchase of *Broom and Broom Corn News* by Don and Linda Rankin.

The last issue of *Broom and Broom Corn News* was March 6, 1982. The following week the publication was listed as *Broom, Brush & Mop Magazine*. Don Rankin discussed the changes taking place in the broomcorn industry: "Most broomcorn is now grown in Mexico and imported by the United States. A large number of small broom shops have evolved into fewer, but considerably larger and more financially sound, broom manufacturers. A number of broom manufacturers have also expanded into mop manufacturing."[1]

BBM continues today, reporting on conventions, meetings, and trade shows. They have numerous advertisers and report on the latest imports/exports of raw materials, finished goods, and trends.

An Industry of Heritage Fathers and Sons

In many areas the broom industry is made up of a number of father and son teams, demonstrating the continuity of the industry, as the knowledge of the father is passed to the son. Thus, the feeling of a close-knit fraternity and an extremely high expertise in this unique business is maintained. In a number of cases it is being passed to third or even fourth generations in active management in the broom industry, as with the Pelton family. Bart Pelton of PelRay International, in San Antonio, Texas,

Daconite cartoon advertisement, private collection. *Courtesy of Bart Pelton*

Daconite cartoon, private collection. *Courtesy of Bart Pelton*

Ready for sales on the streets of Lindsay, Oklahoma, 1910. *Courtesy of Bart Pelton*

Mr. Pelton ready for sales. *Courtesy of Bart Pelton*

Daconite carton, private collection. *Courtesy of Bart Pelton*

has been sharing his expertise with his daughter, a fourth generation Pelton. Through the family history of Bart Pelton and Ray LeBlanc, PelRay can trace its record of unparalleled customer service back to 1905, when Bart's grandfather, Harve Pelton, started Western Warehouse, later known as Western Broom Supply Company and National Broomcorn Company, in Wichita, Kansas. In those early years, the company focused on supplying broomcorn to broom factories. The broom industry was labor intensive and required little technology. The Peltons were dependent on family labor for their success throughout the history of their companies. The industry and the Peltons were only slightly affected by new technology that developed in the twentieth century. Industry resistance to higher worker wages and new labor practices only further encouraged low tech practices. Later the company added handles and mop yarn to better serve the cleaning industry. In 1946, Harve Pelton hired Francis "Rudy" LeBlanc to manage a new branch in Birmingham, Alabama, known as Southern States Supply Company. Bart Pelton and Ray LeBlanc joined the company in 1977, in very different capacities: Ray as a bilingual broomcorn buyer and Bart as controller. Both men were in the right place at the right time to move into the family business. Ray LeBlanc moved from Monterrey, Mexico, to manage the Laredo, Texas, warehouse until he recruited David McGee in 1986, to be the Laredo branch manager. When the Laredo warehouse closed in 2007, David joined Ray in San Antonio, where PelRay continues to have its operations. David now works in sales alongside Bart and Ray, who also wear second hats as president and COO, respectively. PelRay now has a distribution agreement with Italian and Mexican manufacturers of metal handles and angle brooms. PelRay's sister company, American Wood Champions, is certified by the Sustainable Forestry Initiative (SFI). Bart Pelton explains, "The SFI certifies that handles and other wood products are produced in a renewable and environmentally sensitive fashion. This is a significant advantage for our customers who supply the retail trade."

In the early 1990s, broom factories in the United States lobbied against tariff reductions for foreign-made brooms, which took place over several years, but the North American Free Trade Agreement (NAFTA) with Canada and Mexico was implemented January 1, 1994.

Today, PelRay International, LLC distributes not only broomcorn, but wood and metal handles, yucca fiber (bear grass), palmyra, Tampico fiber, and mop yarn, as well as mop and broom hardware. Ray LeBlanc notes the most critical element of the company's success over its long history is due to its quality of customer service. The company's mission is "Achieving Success through Integrity, Service and Quality," and it shows. The Pelton's fourth generation has now joined the company, and she is now vice president of business development.

The Monahan family has been involved in the broom business for well over 130 years. In the late 1800s, Patrick Henry Monahan, an immigrant from Loughrea, Ireland, was one of the first broomcorn brokers to set up shop in Illinois. Patrick Monahan had traveled around the East Coast for a number of years before settling in Arcola in the 1860s. In 1867, Monahan set up shop as a broomcorn broker. This was over one hundred years before the invention of broomcorn processing (the preparation of broomcorn for use by manufacturers, an innovation introduced in the 1960s by Tim Monahan), so brokers were also asked to shop for the type of crops that would best fit the needs of individual manufacturers. What began in 1922 as a small domestic broomcorn brokerage firm has grown over its eight decades into a worldwide supplier of all the parts needed to put together a broom, brush, or mop. Three third-generation grandsons of the Monahan family operate the business. "In high school, or even in late grade school, we worked in the warehouses during the summer—unloading broomcorn," Jim Monahan said. "In high school, we were sent to some of the broomcorn growing fields in Colorado, Oklahoma, and South Texas. We grew up around broomcorn

Broom handles. *Courtesy of Bart Pelton*

Monahan Partners. *Photo courtesy of Pat Monahan*

The goal of NAFTA was to eliminate barriers to trade and investment between the US, Canada, and Mexico. The implementation of NAFTA brought the immediate elimination of tariffs on more than one-half of Mexico's exports to the US and more than one-third of US exports to Mexico. Within ten years of the implementation of the agreement, all US-Mexico tariffs would be eliminated except for some US agricultural exports to Mexico that were to be phased out within fifteen years.2

Before NAFTA, the import duty on Mexican corn brooms was thirty-two percent, with a minimum tariff of $0.32 each (mostly on low price whisk brooms). When NAFTA started, the duty immediately dropped to twenty-two percent, and the first 1.2 million brooms each year (the quota) were duty free. Whisk brooms and brooms costing under $0.96 each were duty-free. This allegedly made it easy to cheat on the tariff by submitting fake import invoices to US Customs. The duty was gradually reduced and eliminated starting in 2004. Also, the Mexican peso was devalued in 1994, giving Mexican broom makers an even larger cost advantage over US broom makers. As a result, many US broom businesses shut down their corn broom manufacturing and started importing Mexican made brooms. Mexican brooms started replacing US brooms at Walmart, Home Depot, and other retailers. US broomcorn consumption has declined ninety percent since NAFTA started.3

and were in the broom and mop business ever since we were old enough to think about it."

R. E. Caddy & Company, Inc., of Greensboro, North Carolina, has been in business fifty-eight years as a raw material distributor. The company serves broom, brush, and mop manufacturers across the United States, Canada, and other countries. R. E. Caddy & Company, Inc., was founded in 1958 by the late Earl Caddy, who purchased the East Coast branch of the John L. Denning Company, a large broomcorn supplier at the time. Earl Caddy had worked twelve years for the John L. Denning Company prior to starting on his own. With loyal customers and the assistance and friendship of would-be competitors, Caddy's new adventure as a broomcorn dealer flourished. It also took him to various global locations in search of better product. In 1961, he made a business trip to Italy. "The purpose of the Italy trip was to start the first dyed broomcorn production. The operation was set up in one day, and within two days of that we had some of the best, brightest dyed red and green colored broomcorn that I'd ever seen," explained Earl Caddy. In the late 1960s, Caddy began to make frequent trips to Mexico to purchase broomcorn. It was not until his son, Richard, was a freshman in college that he started going to Mexico with his father. In 1983, after twenty-five years of running his own business, Earl Caddy gladly accepted a promotion to chairman of the board and welcomed his son, Richard Caddy, who had been working in public administration in Iowa, as the new president of the company. "It takes an awful lot of hard work to operate a small company. My dad didn't delegate much to anybody over the years when he ran the business. But because he had so much knowledge of the industry, by the time I started, I had an encyclopedia of broomcorn working right across the desk from me. He made it very easy to make the transition into the business and we always got along well," says Richard.

While visiting the Amana Colonies in Iowa, at the Broom & Basket Shop, Joanna Schanz showed me a broom poem. It was written in German, but she had their broom maker, Harry Leonhardt, translate it for this book. Harry was their broom maker for fifteen years. He retired at age 94, only because he was going blind.

Monument in Padova, Italy, designed and built by the Rossetto family of broom makers. *Courtesy of PelRay International LLC*

ODE TO THE BROOM
If you buy a broom I would,
Give you advise that's very good.
If you will hang it on the wall
And keep it in your closet tall,
And leave it there for future use,
It will stay new, with no abuse.
If later then the time will come,
When all the other brooms are done,
Then, with a smile you go and get,
Your brand new broom—but yet,
You should treat it with respect
And should remember that in fact,
How few Broom Makers there are today,
Who care to make the broom O.K.
For if you buy one in the store,
The broom is not, but the price is more.
Therefore, we will always strive,
To give the broom the longest life.
Whoever follows this advice,
Will, I believe, benefit twice,
The new broom will sweep so clean,
As anything you've ever seen,
Whoso does not heed this plan,
Will have to buy a broom again.
Emilie Hahn—Author
Harry A. Leonhardt—Translator

CHAPTER SEVEN

Photo Gallery

World's largest broom, Padua, Italy. *Photo courtesy of PelRay International, LLC*

JoAnn Kelly Catsos, wedding broom. *Courtesy of JoAnn Kelly Catsos*

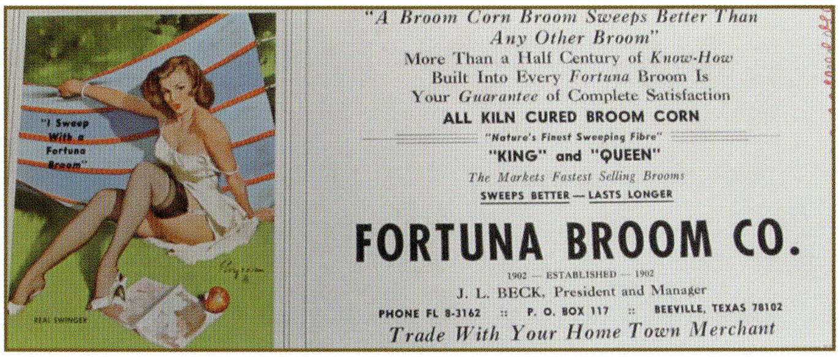

Fortuna Broom Co. advertisement , private collection.
Courtesy of Bart Pelton

Fortuna Broom Co. advertisement , private collection.
Courtesy of Bart Pelton

Broom handle label, private collection. *Courtesy of Bart Pelton*

Broom handle label, private collection. *Courtesy of Bart Pelton*

Broom handle label, private collection. *Courtesy of Bart Pelton*

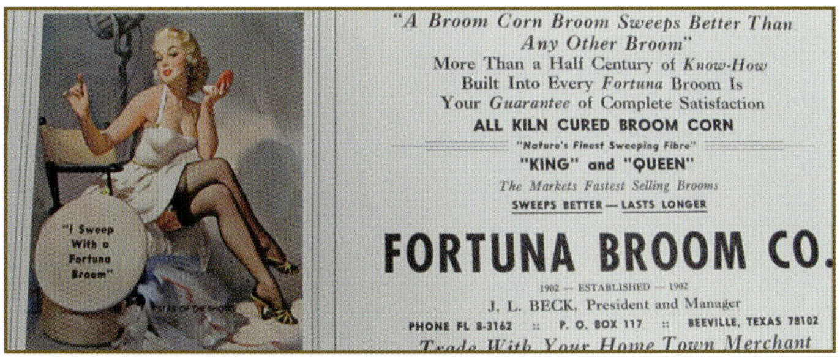

Fortuna Broom Co. advertisement , private collection.
Courtesy of Bart Pelton

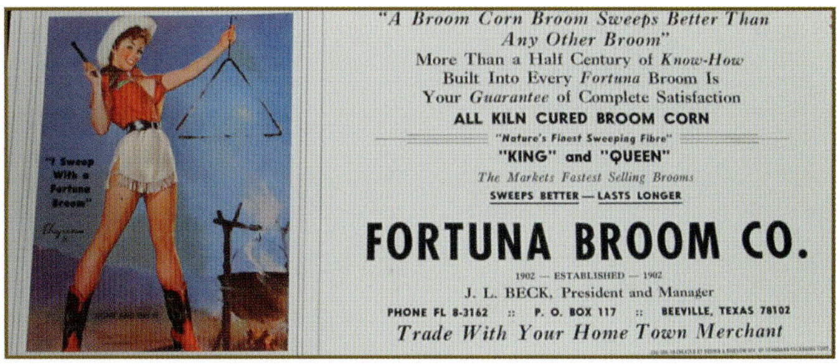

Fortuna Broom Co. advertisement , private collection.
Courtesy of Bart Pelton

Bev Larson, angled whisk broom. *Courtesy of Bev Larson*

Bev Larson, plaiting. *Courtesy Bev Larson*

Jeanne Dudley, "Black Rose" whisk, natural/dyed whisk brooms. *Courtesy of Jeanne Dudley*

Karen Hobbs, "San" whisk. *Courtesy of Maggie Lane Studio*

Joanna Schanz, "Sideliner" with "Double Sideliner" brooms. *Courtesy of Broom & Basket Shop, West Amana, Iowa*

Leesa Thompson, "American" turkey wing. *Courtesy of Thompsons Brooms*

Karen Hobbs, "Bear" whisk broom. *Courtesy of Maggie Lane Studio*

Karen Hobbs, angel wing whisk broom with plaiting. *Courtesy of Maggie Lane Studio*

Leesa Thompson, "Black Turkey Wing" whisk with seeds. *Courtesy of Thompsons Brooms*

Broom woven in the People's Republic of China, private collection. *Courtesy of Maggie Lane Studio*

Leesa Thompson, brown-beaded turkey wing whisk. *Courtesy of Thompsons Brooms*

Bobbie McClure, brush woven with palmyra, private collection. *Courtesy of Maggie Lane Studio*

Carvel Morgan, kitchen brooms. *Courtesy of Carvel Morgan, Davenport, Iowa*

Mark Hendry, "Brussel Sprout Cane" broom. *Courtesy of Mark G. Hendry, Photo by John Polak*

Carvel Morgan, various brooms. *Courtesy of Carvel Morgan, Davenport, Iowa*

Carvel Morgan, whisk brooms. *Courtesy of Carvel Morgan, Davenport, Iowa*

"Little" John Holzwart, guitar broom. *Photo courtesy of "Little" John Holzwart*

Leesa and Wayne Thompson, close up of sweeper. *Courtesy of Thompsons Brooms*

Leesa and Wayne Thompson, child's broom. *Courtesy of Thompsons Brooms*

Karen Hobbs, "Eagle Parlor" broom. *Courtesy of Maggie Lane Studio*

Marlow Gates, "Double Bittersweet Fairy Duster." *Courtesy of Friendswood Brooms*

Karen Hobbs, gourd whisk broom. *Courtesy of Maggie Lane Studio*

Karen Hobbs, hearth broom with carved handle. *Courtesy of Maggie Lane Studio*

Karen Hobbs, Santa whisk broom. *Courtesy of Maggie Lane Studio*

Ed Harris, European round hearth broom. *Courtesy of Haydenville Broomworks, Photo by John Polak*

Karen Hobbs, "Blue" hawk tail whisk. *Courtesy of Maggie Lane Studio*

Peter Werner, hawk tail whisk. *Courtesy of Clean Sweep, Black Mountain, North Carolina*

Karen Hobbs, pot scrubber. *Courtesy of Maggie Lane Studio*

Bev Larson, flat broom. *Courtesy of Bev Larson*

Bev Larson, angel wing whisk. *Courtesy of Bev Larson*

Wayne Thompson, "Golden Boy" kitchen broom. *Courtesy of Thompsons Brooms*

"Little" John Holzwart, "Crutch" broom. *Photo courtesy of "Little" John Holzwart*

Bev Larson, turkey wing whisk. *Courtesy of Bev Larson*

Karen Hobbs, "King Sweeper" broom. *Courtesy of Maggie Lane Studio*

Bev Larson, corn silkers. *Courtesy of Bev Larson*

Karen Hobbs, animal whisk brooms. *Courtesy of Maggie Lane Studio*

Karen Hobbs, "Bronze" hawk tail whisk. *Courtesy of Maggie Lane Studio*

Beth and John Lovin, hearth broom with forged handle. *Courtesy of John and Beth Lovin*

Karen Hobbs, multicolored whisk brooms. *Courtesy of Maggie Lane Studio*

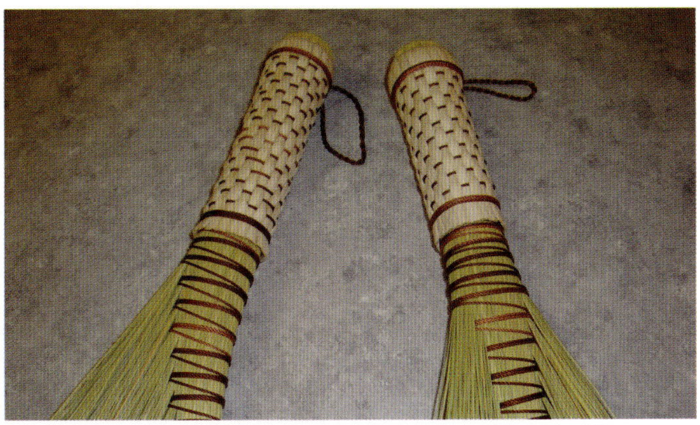

Jackie Thomas, whisk brooms. *Courtesy of Jackie Thomas*

Wayne and Leesa Thompson, lime green kitchen broom. *Courtesy of Thompsons Brooms*

Marlow Gates, "May the Circle. . . ." *Courtesy of Friendswood Brooms*

Ed Harris, mini whisk brooms. *Courtesy of Haydenville Broomworks, Photo by John Polak*

Charlotte Baker, kitchen broom. *Courtesy of Charlotte Baker*

Charlotte Baker, curved handle broom. *Courtesy of Charlotte Baker*

Charlotte Baker, whisk broom. *Courtesy of Charlotte Baker*

Charlotte Baker, cobweb and kitchen brooms. *Courtesy of Charlotte Baker*

Charlotte Baker, hawk tail whisk broom. *Courtesy of Charlotte Baker*

Charlotte Baker, turkey wing whisk broom. *Courtesy of Charlotte Baker*

Karen Hobbs, "Lonesome Dove" quidditch broom. *Courtesy of Maggie Lane Studio*

Karen Hobbs, multi-color angel wing whisk. *Courtesy of Maggie Lane Studio*

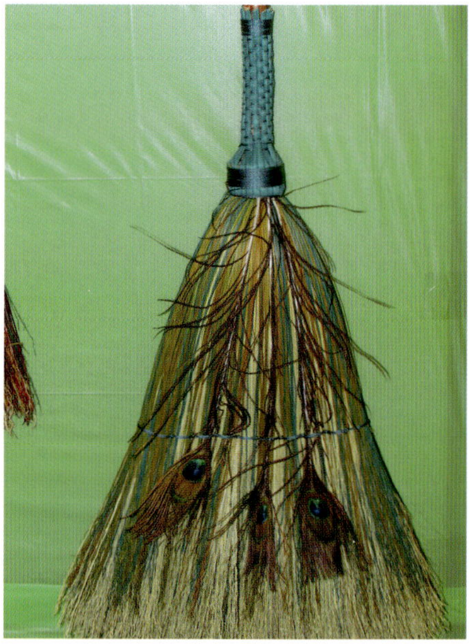

Bev Larson, "Peacock" kitchen broom. *Courtesy of Bev Larson*

Leesa Thompson, multi-plait whisk broom. *Courtesy of Thompsons Brooms*

Fritz W. Musser, turkey wing and whisk brooms. *Courtesy of Fritz Musser*

Wayne and Leesa Thompson, red/green sweeper. *Courtesy of Thompsons Brooms*

Fritz W. Musser, small whisk brooms. *Courtesy of Fritz W. Musser*

Bev Larson, "The Broom Lady" broom rack. *Courtesy of Bev Larson*

"Aunt Jemima" vintage clothes brush, private collection. *Courtesy of Maggie Lane Studio*

Karen Hobbs, turkey, whisk, and cake tester. *Courtesy of Maggie Lane Studio*

Ed Harris, pot scrubbers. *Courtesy of Haydenville Broomworks, Photo by John Polak*

Vintage whisk, private collection. *Courtesy of Maggie Lane Studio*

Fritz W. Musser, kitchen brooms. *Courtesy of Fritz W. Musser*

"The Queen of Brooms" broom handle label, private collection. *Courtesy of Bart Pelton*

Vintage clothes brush, private collection. *Courtesy of Maggie Lane Studio*

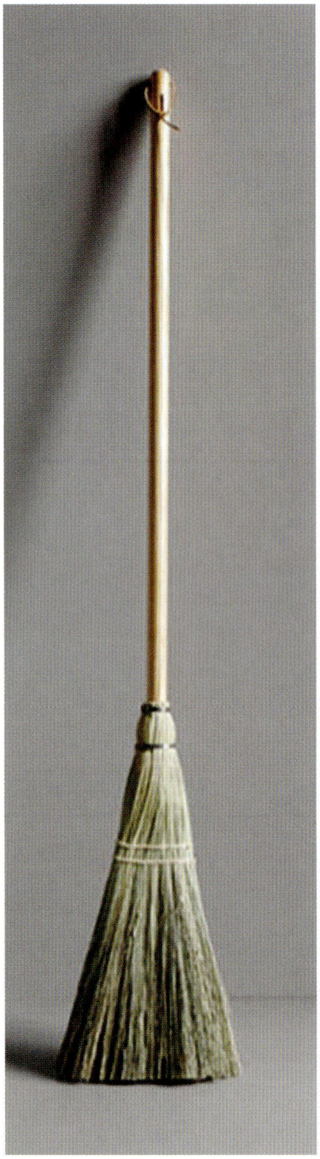

Ed Harris, Shaker broom. *Courtesy of Haydenville Broomworks, Photo by John Polak*

Karen Hobbs, red turkey wing whisk. *Courtesy of Maggie Lane Studio*

Ralph Gates, "Strange and Off Putting" antler broom. *Courtesy of Friendswood Brooms*

Karen Hobbs, various tall brooms. *Courtesy of Maggie Lane Studio*

Ed Harris, turkey wing brooms. *Courtesy of Haydenville Broomworks, Photo by John Polak*

Karen Hobbs, turkey wing assembled with wire. *Courtesy of Maggie Lane Studio*

Karen Hobbs, besom broom. *Courtesy Maggie Lane Studio*

Peter Werner, wedding broom. *Courtesy of Peter Werner, Clean Sweep, Black Mountain, North Carolina*

Karen Hobbs, willow hearth broom. *Courtesy of Maggie Lane Studio*

Karen Hobbs, whisk brooms. *Courtesy of Maggie Lane Studio*

Peter Werner, whisk broom. *Courtesy of Peter Werner, Clean Sweep, Black Mountain, North Carolina*

"Little" John Holzwart, full plaited brooms. *Courtesy of "Little" John Holzwart*

Chris Robbins, "The Forest Gnome" broom. *Courtesy of Chris Robbins, Berea, Kentucky*

Chris Robbins, "Brawny Mountain" whisk broom. *Courtesy of Chris Robbins, Berea, Kentucky*

Chris Robbins, "Shaker Braid" broom. *Courtesy of Chris Robbins, Berea, Kentucky*

Chris Robbins, "Will-O-Wisp" broom. *Courtesy of Chris Robbins, Berea, Kentucky*

Chris Robbins, "Cindersweep" broom. *Courtesy of Chris Robbins, Berea, Kentucky*

Chris Robbins, "Hearthsweep" broom. *Courtesy of Chris Robbins, Berea, Kentucky*

Marlow Gates, "Wedding Broom." *Courtesy of Friendswood Brooms*

Marlow Gates, "Roots." *Courtesy of Friendswood Brooms*

"Little" John Holzwart, hearth brooms. *Courtesy of "Little" John Holzwart*

Marlow Gates, "As Above, So Below." *Courtesy of Friendswood Brooms*

"Little" John Holzwart, kitchen broom. *Courtesy of "Little" John Holzwart*

Hawaiian whisk broom, purchased on the side of a road in Maui. *Courtesy of Maggie Lane Studio*

Karen Hobbs, cake tester. *Courtesy of Maggie Lane Studio*

Daniel Z. Stoltzfus, wall-mounted cake tester with poem. *Courtesy of Maggie Lane Studio*

Dale DeLong, carved broom handles. *Courtesy of Dale DeLong, Spirits in the Wood, Photo by Claudie Parson*

Daniel Z. Stoltzfus, wall-mounted broom holder. *Courtesy of Maggie Lane Studio*

Vintage Flo-Rex whisk broom. *Courtesy of Maggie Lane Studio*

Vintage clothes brush. *Courtesy of Maggie Lane Studio*

Claudie Parson, wedding broom. *Courtesy of Sunflower Broom Shop*

Claudie Parson, wedding broom. *Courtesy of Sunflower Broom Shop*

Certificate from the 1900s for the purchase of stock in the Alice Broom Corn Drying Co., located in Alice, Texas. *Courtesy of Maggie Lane Studio*

Karen Hobbs, sweeper broom, made with Ron Cox at Davis Mountain Broom Shop. *Courtesy of Maggie Lane Studio*

Seed broom, unknown artist. *Courtesy of Maggie Lane Studio*

Broom trivet. *Courtesy of Maggie Lane Studio*

Trivet, brooms and birds. *Courtesy of Maggie Lane Studio*

Leesa and Wayne Thompson whisk brooms. *Courtesy of Thompsons Brooms*

Leesa Thompson, cobweb brooms. *Courtesy of Thompsons Brooms*

Leesa and Wayne Thompson, hearth brooms. *Courtesy of Thompsons Brooms*

Leesa and Wayne Thompson, sweeper brooms. *Courtesy of Thompsons Brooms*

Leesa Thompson, plaited turkey wings. *Courtesy of Thompsons Brooms*

Vintage clothes brush. *Courtesy of Maggie Lane Studio*

CHAPTER EIGHT

Care of the Broom

Take reasonable care of your broom and you will lighten your work. A good broom is much easier to work with.

- Do not store your broom standing on the sweeping end; it bends and warps the straws.
- A little bit of water or dampness never hurts a broom if you shake it thoroughly and hang it up or stand it on the stick end.
- Do not keep your broom in a place that is hot and dry; it makes the straw brittle and stiff.
- When the first three inches or so are worn down, discard the broom or use it only to scrub basement floors. A worn broom takes twice the energy to do half the work.
- Buy only the best quality broomcorn brooms and whisk brooms—they cost little or nothing more.[1]
- Do not use soaps or harsh chemicals on your brooms, as it will remove the natural wax coating of the broomcorn; it will then become dry and brittle.
- If the ends become flared, dip them in warm water twenty to thirty minutes. Wrap the end of the broom with a thin piece of cloth and hang it on the wall overnight. Remove the next morning and it is good as new again.
- Keeping your broom out of direct sunlight will prolong the natural colors.
- Sweeping with alternative sides and corners of a broom helps it wear evenly.[2]

Brooms are best for:

- Sweeping wood, tile, linoleum, cement, and any other kind of floor
- Getting dirt out of carpets and making the nap look like new after it has been beaten down by feet and vacuum cleaners
- Cleaning dust and cobwebs off walls and ceilings
- Sweeping light snow and cut grass from sidewalks and steps
- Retrieving clothes from under beds
- Shampooing rugs
- Props for snowmen
- Beating rugs
- Knocking wasp nests from under house eaves
- Gifts for kitchen or closet bridal showers
- Completing a witch's costume for Halloween
- Cleaning fireplaces

Whisk brooms are great for:

- Sweeping boat and car interiors
- Brushing lint off clothes and hats—put a little hook on your ironing board and keep one handy when ironing clothes or linens
- Cleaning work surfaces in your wood working shop
- Cleaning inside corners of upholstered furniture or floors when trimmed into a V-shape
- Creating a "brushed" design when painting walls and ceilings
- Cleaning stair carpeting
- Removing hair and lint from small throw rugs
- Taking dry mud or snow off dogs and cats

CHAPTER NINE

Patterns

Grouping of brooms. *Courtesy of Maggie Lane Studio*

The broom patterns in this chapter include step-by-step photographs and written instructions I have used for teaching purposes at conventions and retreats. They are basic steps to help you learn the beginning techniques of broom making. Natural broomcorn is used in the pictures. Adding a small amount of dyed hurl to brooms can be quite striking. When not being used, store broomcorn or hurl in a cool, dry, well-ventilated area away from direct sunlight. I keep mine covered, because direct sunlight will eventually discolor broomcorn and yellow it. (Normally fresh broomcorn has a greenish color to it. Broomcorn grown in Hungary is more yellow and coarser than broomcorn grown in Mexico because of the environment.)

For the purpose of these patterns, I teach with a tying block held under my feet with twine wound in the middle. That is how I learned at John Campbell Folk School years ago, it is easy to travel teach with, and students take home what they do not use.

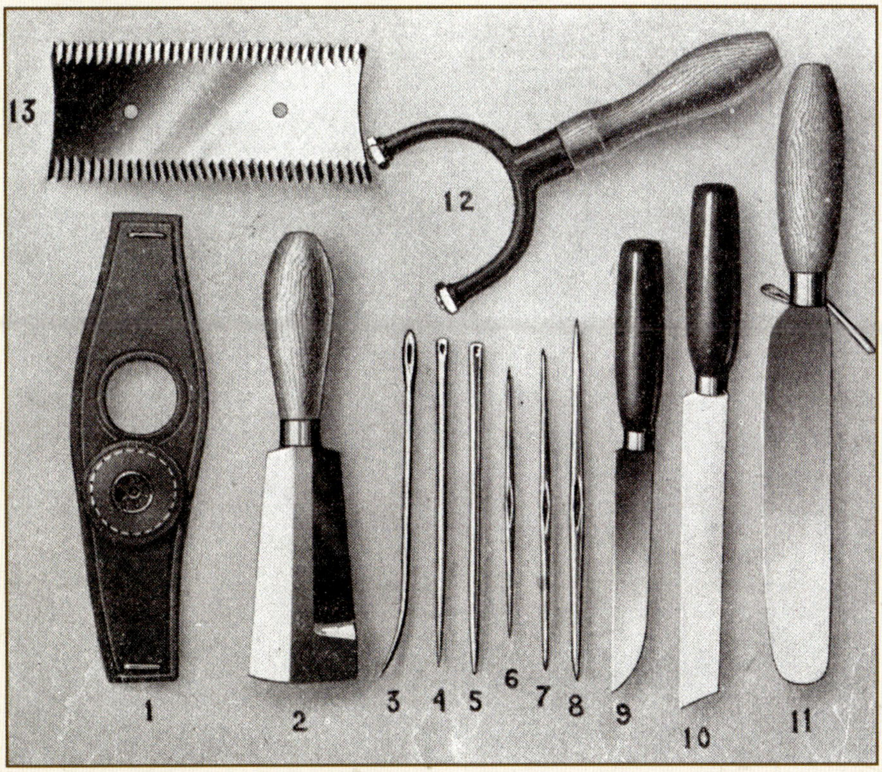

Broom making tools of yesteryear, private collection. *Courtesy of Bart Pelton*

Let us first take a look at some of the tools that are used in broom making. The first picture shows traditional tools used.

1. **Sewing Cuff:** for protecting the palms of your hands when the broom is being held in a sewing press and using a double pointed needle. The hole for the twine is in the center of the needle.
2. **Pounder:** when making brooms on a kick winder, the pounder is used to aid tightening the wire at various stages. The flat side of the pounder is used to drive staples and nails.
3. **Bunching Needle:** a curved needle for sewing brooms by hand. Originally used for binding together bunches of brooms for shipment.

4. & 5. **Eyed Needles:** for sewing brooms by hand.

6. 7. & 8. **Double Pointed Needles:** used when brooms are held in a broom press and sewn.

9. **String Knife:** super sharp and great for trimming sewing twine. While making Shaker style, the string knife is good for cutting single pieces of broom hurl to then place back into the broom.
10. **Serrated Knife:** great for cutting broom hurl when a whisk broom is complete.
11. **Broad Knife:** good for cutting the broom off when terminating the end. It can be turned at an angle at the top of broomcorn to do what is called a "rundown." This angles the broomcorn to prepare to add the next layer.
12. **Handle to #13.**
13. **Hand Scraper:** used for removing the seeds from broomcorn.

Tools used in classroom setting. *Photo courtesy of Zachary Alan Photography*

Next are the tools used in a classroom setting

- **Twine:** There are numerous brands of twine. A lot depends on if the broom maker is doing it as a hobby, making just a few brooms every now and then, or starting with a kick winder and making production brooms. For this purpose I use #18 tarred twine. It does not slip and has tooth to it. It can be purchased from boat supply companies.
- **Serrated Knife:** for cutting the end of whisk brooms at completion.
- **Large Vise:** for holding the shape of larger brooms while sewing flat.
- **Small Vise:** for holding whisk brooms or smaller hearth brooms while sewing flat.
- **Various Sewing Needles:** Flat with a hole in the middle for sewing the broom while being held in a broom press.
- **Stainless Steel Needle:** with eye in one end I had made for classroom use. Flat needles can be purchased from PelRay International, LLC.
- **Zip Tie:** To hold hurl while cutting ends; otherwise they go everywhere.
- **Scissors/shears:** because of their length, these are great for cutting the end of twine when finishing a broom and trimming stalks. They have comfortable plastic handles with small, sharply pointed tips. They do not rust, and are available from most basketry suppliers.
- **Needle Nose Pliers:** these are used to help thread a hanger through a handle and ensure knots are tied.
- **Flat Awl:** great for aiding with plaiting. The awl is also used to bury the twine.
- **Knife:** a single sharp knife is needed for splitting stalks.

There are various ways to tie brooms. Here you will see pictures of Wayne Thompson tying a broom with a kick winder.

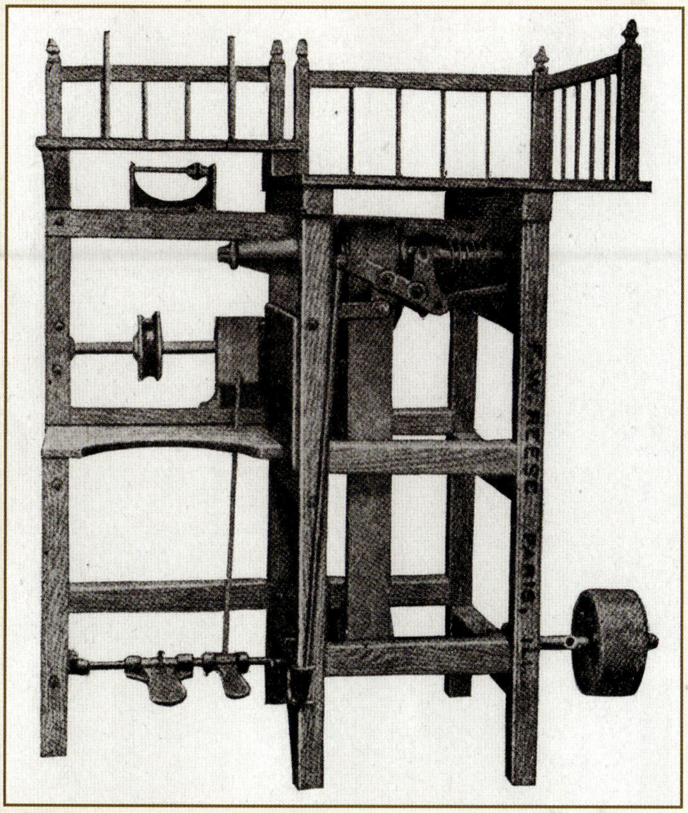

Treadle kick winder, private collection. *Courtesy of Bart Pelton*

Kick winder new from Mexico. *Courtesy of Karen Hobbs*

Kick winder used at Amana Colonies. *Courtesy of Karen Hobbs*

When using a kick winder, the handle is first placed into the chuck. *Courtesy of Karen Hobbs*

The first layer of hurl is then wound on to the handle. *Courtesy of Karen Hobbs*

The wire is then turned up the handle a short way. *Courtesy of Karen Hobbs*

A second layer of hurl is added next; wire is turned up and excess is cut off with a broad knife. *Courtesy of Karen Hobbs*

The third layer is added in the same manner. At times a fourth layer of color is then added with wire running in a decorative manner, and a nail is driven into the end of the wire; excess hurl is cut off. *Courtesy of Karen Hobbs*

A completed broom at Thompsons Brooms located in Leighton, Alabama. *Courtesy of Karen Hobbs*

A John Simurdak design of the Shaker style broom box. *Courtesy of Maggie Lane Studio*

Another way of tying broomcorn is with a tying wheel. Marlow Gates's father Ralph Gates (of Friendswood Brooms) and another broom maker designed a wheel for under your feet. They started out using the leftover big wooden spools sewing string came on. Traditionally, broom makers used just a stout branch or piece of kindling with a notch cut all the way around. The idea has been around since the Shakers.

Shown is a mobile broom box. It is a modified type of Shaker broom box built by Bill Soetaert of Mountain View, Arkansas. It was modified to include the squirrel cage at the bottom for foot control. This is the one I use, and was made by my therapist after my stroke. He was eager to get me back into my hobbies and the things I enjoyed.

In the picture of class tools, you will notice a tying table I purchased while at the Ozark Folk Center. It has a wheel underneath for your feet, has spaces for two to four colors, and one for wire if desired.

Tying Wheel. *Courtesy of Maggie Lane Studio*

For left-handers, the sequence is reversed: you will hold the broom in your right hand and add broomcorn or hurl with the left.

Turkey Wing Whisk Broom

MATERIALS

- **Broom hurl:** enough that your middle finger and thumbnail overlap, approximately 1 to 1 1¤2 inches diameter. (Hurl is broomcorn without the stalk.)
- **Nylon twine:** approximately ten yards
- Tying block: fifteen inches long to wrap twine on and use under your feet to tie corn. (A piece of one inch by two inch wood)
- Basket or pruning shears
- Serrated knife or pocket knife

PLEASE NOTE: Once you start tying this broom, you cannot stop until finished. It is a continuous wrap. Have all tools within reach.

INSTRUCTIONS

Cut two pieces from the twine: one for the hanger (approximately twenty inches) and one for the pull cord (approximately sixteen inches). Fold both in half and tie the loose ends together. Set these aside for later. You could also use leather or other hangers if desired.

Drill a hole in the center of the tying block. Knot the twine through the hole and wrap the twine around it in the center, leaving room for your feet at both ends. Wrap approximately nine to twelve yards of twine around the stick.

Divide your hurl into eleven piles on a table next to you.

Lay your tying block under your feet so the twine comes from underneath and next to you.

Take your final bundle, which is the largest (tap the wispy ends on the table to get them even each time you pick up a pile) and place it in your non-dominant hand with the soft/wispy ends facing your dominant hand. Slip the twine through the middle of the hurl about three to four inches from the wispy end, leaving roughly a two-inch tail on the twine. Wrap toward yourself, going around the bundle once. Then place the tail of the twine over the wrap and toward your non-dominant hand. Wrap tightly three more times going up the hurl, over this tail, toward your non-dominant hand. This catches and locks the end of the twine. This tail will be covered with the side addition.

Now, holding hurl with your non-dominant hand, "V"up the twine about half an inch on the side. Pick up the next pile of hurl on top and add it to this side of your broom, going under the "V." Wrap three times. Again, "V" up half an inch and add another pile on the side, then wrap three times. You will be adding on the side four to six times, depending on your piles.

After you have wrapped three times with the last addition, continue the "V" up and three wraps for as long as you want your handle to be. The "V" side is usually on the back, but occasionally I make it to the front.

When you are at the top on the back side, place your hanger under the first wrap of the last three-wrap cycle. After placing your hanger, wrap three times. Now place the rip cord that you tied earlier with the loop facing the handle end. Wrap over this pull string three or four more times. Hold the last wrap with your thumb, then cut two to three inches long. Place the end through the pull loop and hold again with your thumb. With your dominant hand pull the rip cord, thus pulling the end of the twine under the wraps to secure the end. Cut to approximately half an inch, *no shorter*! Using an awl, bury the end down in the hurl of your broom.

Secure the extra handle ends of the hurl with a zip tie; this will save a mess when cutting. Trim the sweeping end either straight across or slightly rounded, being aware not to cut too much of the "sweeper" off (this is the small, wispy ends of the hurl).

Pattern photos pages 51–102 courtesy of Zachary Alan Photography

1 Divide the ten ounce bundle of hurl in half, then into four piles and five piles.

2 The piles stacked in front of you.

3 Bring the twine up through the middle of the hurl approximately three to four inches from the wispy end.

4 Lock the end of the twine by going under, then over it.

5 After locking the end of the twine, make three (3) tight wraps, stopping where the twine came out.

6 The first "V" up will be directly over the end of the twine.

7 The first addition of hurl will be at the "V," keeping it on the side covering the end of the twine and not letting it roll around to the top or other side.

8 Again, wrapping three (3) times around, stopping at the side where you added hurl.

9 When wrapping, your twine should meet the "V" to make a straight line. There should be straight lines next to you and there should be "Vs" away from you where you are adding the hurl each time.

10 "V" up, and add another pile, adding under your twine.

11 Add hurl, keeping it on the side. The broom should be flat at this point.

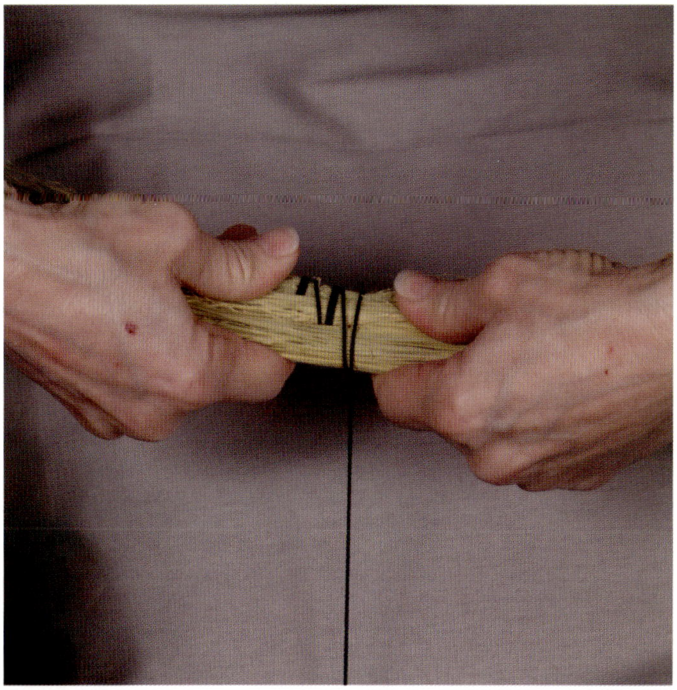

12 Wrap to meet the "V," then continue making the three (3) wraps tightly.

13 Continue adding the piles with the "V" up then three (3) wraps.

14 One side should look like straight lines.

15 The other side will have "V" ups. Continue with the "V" ups and three wraps after the piles have been added to form the handle.

16 When the handle is long enough, place the rip cord with loop toward the handle, under the twine.

17 Wrap three (3) times, going over the rip cord.

18 With your non-dominant hand, place your thumb on the wraps and cut the twine, leaving about three inches. Place the end through the loop of the rip cord.

19 Keeping your thumb on the wraps, with your dominant hand, pull the rip cord, thus pulling the end of twine underneath the rows of wraps to secure it.

20 Trim twine to one to two inches. Bury the end down into the hurl using an awl.

21 The finished turkey wing.

22 To assist in the curvature of the turkey wing, bend it around your knee.

23 More curve after bending around the knee.

Whisk Brooms, Plaiting the Tops

MATERIALS

- **7 mm flat oval reed:** natural or dyed. Approximately fifteen pieces six to seven inches long *or* Broomcorn stalks split to size
- **Nylon twine:** approximately ten yards
- **Tying block:** fifteen inches long to wrap twine on and use under your feet to tie corn (a piece of one inch by two inch wood)
- Basket or pruning shears
- Serrated knife or pocket knife
- Bucket of water and an old towel. Use warm water if using broomcorn and soak twenty to thirty minutes

INSTRUCTIONS

Soak your seven millimeter reed for five to ten minutes to soften.* (If using broomcorn stalks, soak twenty to thirty minutes in warm water.) Lay out on a towel. Pick up your twine and tie it around the top of your broom tightly just below the four top wraps. If you have not already placed your hanger, lay the hanger twine/leather with the loop end—as long as you like—toward your non-dominant hand on the back side of the broom. Wrap three times toward the handle end. This ensures that you cover these extra wraps when you begin the plaiting/weaving.

You will now begin to add the seven millimeter reed and plait the top of your broom. Begin adding the seven millimeter reed under the wrap with the oval side down next to the broom. Place approximately half an inch under the twine with the long ends toward the hanging loop. As you add the reed, place them close together without overlapping, turn the broom toward you, and continue adding all the way around the handle, keeping it taut.

Note: You want to add an uneven number of seven millimeter reed pieces, trying to get them as close as possible. This allows for continuous plaiting of the handle. If you come up with an even number, you can simply jump two when you get to the back and make a spiral on your handle, or do a twill pattern of sorts.

When all of the reed is in place, wrap around three times very tightly. Angle down 3⁄8 in. and wrap three more times just on top of the short ends to secure them. Starting at the back, gently bend all seven millimeter reeds down toward the sweeping end and wrap three times, stopping in the back just one piece past the beginning.

Now begin the over/under of plaiting or weaving. Keep this tight. Go over one reed and under the next, over one, under one, etc. Continue around, spiraling down until the plaiting is as long as you wish, stopping in the back where you started.

Again place the pull cord under the twine with the loop toward the wispy end; wrap three times and cut, holding the end with your thumb. Place the twine end into the loop and pull. Cut the end to half an inch and tuck under the seven millimeter reed to hide and secure.

Using a serrated knife or pocket knife, carefully trim the handle end just above the seven millimeter plaiting, being careful not to cut the hanging loop. Trim the sweeping end either straight across or slightly rounded.

*Where I talk about seven millimeter reed, you can do the same using broomcorn stalks.

1 Tie the twine around the top of the whisk broom.

2 Wrap a couple times around, catching the knot, then spiral up to the top, above the last row of wraps. Place your hanger in the back of your broom and wrap tightly three (3) times around, stopping in the back.

3 Begin placing the first 7 mm reed under the twine. Here the first one is being placed on top of the hanger.

4 Continue placing the 7 mm reeds under the twine side-by-side; do not allow to overlap.

5 Once the 7 mm reeds are all the way around, wrap three (3) times.

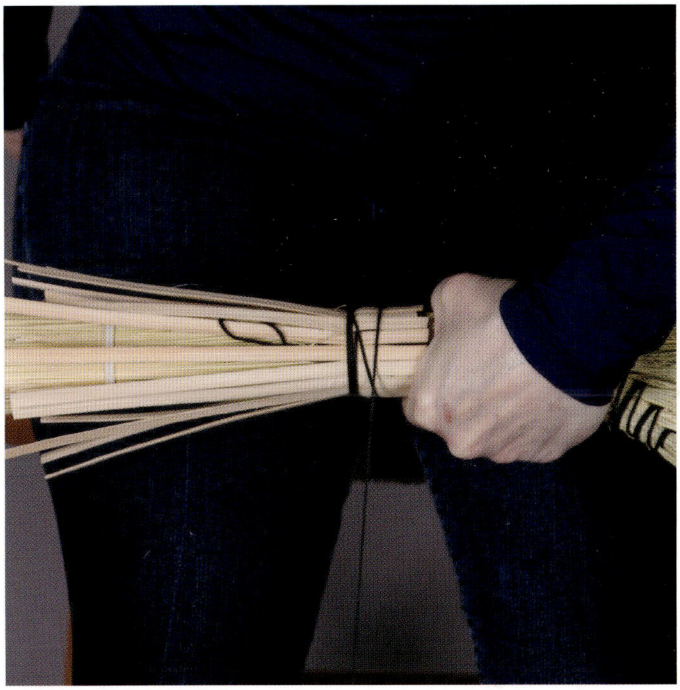

6 Spiral down a half inch and wrap three (3) more times, stopping in the back.

7 At the back, begin to bend the 7 mm reeds down, under the twine.

8 Tug on the 7 mm reed to ensure it is straight and taught.

9 Continue all the way around until the back is reached.

10 Once you are at the back, make sure the twine is in line and wrap three (3) times tightly without overlapping.

11 Starting at the back, begin the over/under weave of plaiting.

12 An awl is sometimes helpful to assist the twine in staying straight and up close to the wraps.

13 The rows will naturally spiral as the 7 mm reeds are plaited. Try to keep the plaiting at a consistent spacing.

14 The plaiting may continue as long as there is enough length on the 7 mm reeds. There needs to be at least 1 1⁄2 in. at the end for final wraps and for securing the twine.

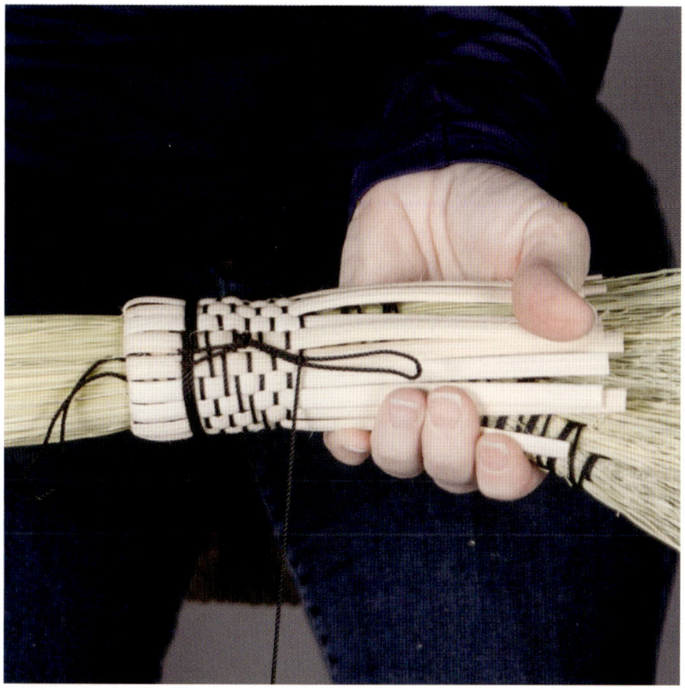

15 At the end of plaiting, place the rip cord under the twine with the loop toward the broom end.

16 Make three (3) tight wraps over the rip cord, careful not to overlap. With your thumb on the twine, cut the cord and place the end through the loop. Pull the loop under the rows of wraps, securing the twine. Trim and bury under a row of plaiting.

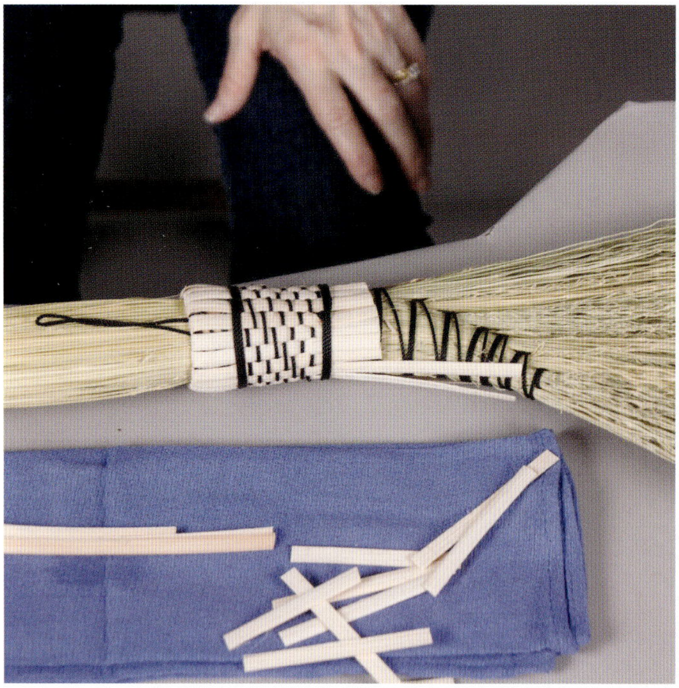

17 Trim ends no shorter than one inch. The 7 mm reeds will shrink some, and more can be trimmed later.

18 Apply a zip tie, then using a serrated knife, trim the end of the whisk.

19 The end of the knife or a hammer may be used to even the end if need be.

Plaited turkey whisk broom. Broomcorn stalks can also be plaited on whisk brooms; simply soak and split to size.

Angel Wing Whisk Broom

MATERIALS

- **Broom hurl:** enough that your middle finger and thumb nail overlap, approximately 1 to 1 1¤2 in. diameter. (Hurl is broomcorn without the stalk.)
- **Nylon twine:** approximately ten yards
- **7 mm flat oval reed** dyed your favorite color. Approximately fifteen pieces, six to seven inches long
- **Tying block:** fifteen inches long to wrap twine on and use under your feet to tie corn (a piece of one inch by two inch wood)
- Basket or pruning shears
- Serrated knife or pocket knife
- Bucket of water and an old towel

PLEASE NOTE: Once you start tying this broom, you cannot stop until finished. It is a continuous wrap. Have all tools within reach.

INSTRUCTIONS

Cut two pieces from the twine: one for the hanger (approximately ten inches) and one for the rip cord (approximately sixteen inches). Fold both in half and tie the loose ends together. Set these aside for later. You could also use leather or other hangers if desired.

Drill a hole in the center of the tying block. Knot the twine through the hole and wrap the twine around it in the center, leaving room for your feet at both ends. Wrap approximately nine to twelve yards of twine around the stick.

Divide your hurl into thirteen piles on a table next to you (refer to the picture).

If you are going to plait the top, place your seven millimeter reed in water to soak. Usually thirteen to fifteen will go around your whisk broom handle. It is better to soak too many than not enough. You want an uneven number, unless you are doing a twill plait.

Lay your tying block under your feet so the twine comes from underneath and next to you.

Take your final bundle, which is the largest (tap the wispy ends on the table to get them even each time you pick up a pile) and place it in your non-dominant hand with the soft/wispy ends facing your dominant hand. Slip the twine through the middle of the hurl about six to seven inches from the wispy end, leaving approximately a three-inch tail on the twine. Wrap toward yourself, going around the bundle once. Then place the tail of the twine over the wrap and toward your non-dominant hand. Wrap tightly three more times going up the hurl, over this tail, toward your non-dominant hand. This catches and locks the end of the twine. This tail will be covered with the side addition.

Now holding hurl with your non-dominant hand, "V"up the twine about half an inch on the side. Pick up the next pile of hurl on top and add it to this side of your broom, going under the "V." Wrap around that addition and add another pile to the other side. Wrap three times. Again, "V" up half an inch and add two more piles on each side, then wrap three times. You will be adding on the side four times.

After you have wrapped three times with the last addition, continue the "V" up and three wraps for as long as you want your handle to be. The "V" side is usually on the back, but occasionally I make it to the front.

When you are at the top on the back side, place your hanger under the first wrap of the last three-wrap cycle. After placing your hanger, wrap three times.

At this point you can stop for a break and tie off or continue on. If tying off, place rip cord with the loop facing the end of the broom. Wrap over this pull string three or four more times. Hold the last wrap with your thumb and cut two to three inches long. Place the end through the pull loop and hold again with your thumb. With your dominant hand pull the rip cord, thus pulling the end of the twine under the wraps to secure the end. Cut to approximately half an inch, *no shorter*! Bury the end down in the hurl of your broom using an awl.

If you choose to continue on, see the instructions for plaiting the tops of whisk brooms. If you stopped, secure a new cord as you started and wrap three more times, stopping in the back, then continue to plait the top.

1 Divide ten ounces of hurl into thirteen piles. One pile should be slightly larger.

2 Start with the larger pile as the core and bring twine up through the center, four to six inches from the wispy ends.

3 Wrap once toward yourself, leaving the end out.

4 Lay the twine end across the first wrap and wrap three (3) more times tightly.

5 "V" up with your non-dominant hand and add hurl with your dominant hand.

6 Add the first pile under the twine, keeping it on the side under the "V."

7 Keeping the broom flat, roll it toward yourself, adding another pile to the opposite side.

8 Turn toward yourself again and the twine will meet at the "V."

9 Wrap two more wraps, making three (3) total, and "V" up. At this point you have "V," two straight wraps, and "V," and now you are ready to add again.

10 After adding to both sides, wrap two more times tightly.

11 One side of the whisk broom will have straight wraps.

12 The opposite side of the whisk broom will have "V" ups.

13 Continue adding on both sides each time a "V" up is made.

14 After all of the hurl is added, continue the pattern to form the handle.

15 When the handle is long enough, place the hanger under the twine (making sure to center in the back), the rip cord under the twine, and wrap three (3) times tightly, stopping in the back.

16 Place your thumb on the wraps and cut the twine, leaving two to three inches. Place the end through the loop and pull the rip cord, securing the twine under the wraps. Bury a one inch end down in the hurl.

The angel wing whisk broom can be plaited at the top, or the end can be cut off with a serrated knife.

Cobweb Broom

INSTRUCTIONS

Finish the handle to your liking and drill a hole in the tapered end about three inches from that end. Hold your stick against a wall and decide which side will be the back and which the front. I usually sign the back to remind me of my decision. Also drill a hole about three inches from the top to hang with a piece of leather.

Drill a hole in the center of the tying block. Knot the twine through the hole and wrap the twine around it in the center, leaving room for your feet at both ends. Wrap approximately nine to twelve yards of twine around the stick.

Fill your bucket with enough warm water to cover the stalk of the broom corn, usually about twelve inches. Place your chosen corn in the water, stalk down, for twenty minutes.

Cut a piece of the twine approximately sixteen inches, fold it in half, and tie the loose ends together. This will be your rip cord. Set this aside for later and keep it handy.

> When tying on straw, wind toward yourself with the handle to your left, palm up, and with the corn to your right.

When your broomcorn is soft—about twenty minutes—take out the inner row and place it on a table next to you. If doing a double layer cobweb broom, you will concave your stalks and trim them to about three inches. By trimming them they will not show, nor will you have to plait them into the outer layer.

Tie your twine through the hole on your handle and tie a good double knot. Roll the stick toward you—pull—roll—pull—roll—pull, stopping on the back side. You will always do three wraps, stopping on the back side. Keep the tension tight!

Now start adding the broomcorn by placing it *under* the string, just above the hurl. Continue placing them side by side with a slight space between. If you are doing a double-layered broom, place the concave side against the handle. When all the broomcorn is around the handle, wrap three times tightly.

If doing double layer wrap three wraps, then wind up the stalks and back down to start adding the next/outer layer. Add the outer layer as you did the inside. Start in the back, bring the broomcorn from under the twine, and place it side by side all the way around. I usually alternate them between the stalks on the inner row as they seem to lay better.

When your broomcorn is attached, you will now begin to plait the stalk. Go under, over, under, over, etc. Keep plaiting as close as possible. You can only go up as far as the length of the stalk. When you are finished plaiting, place the rip cord made earlier next to the plaiting, knot on the handle side. Wrap three times as tightly as you can. Cut the cord, but hold tight and do not let it loosen, then place it through the loop of the rip cord. Pull the rip cord, pulling the end under the tight three rows of wrapping. Cut the end no shorter than one inch. Use an awl to place the end under a row of weaving.

MATERIALS

- Long broomcorn with stalks: enough to go around the handle without overlapping. You will need two layers around the handle if doing a double thickness, trying for an odd number of broomcorn. Keep each layer tied separately.
- Stick for handle: (3/4 to 1 in. diameter, raw or finished, tapered at one end). Drill a 3/16 in. hole three inches from the end. For the cobweb broom, you will need a long, skinny stick
- Twine: I use tarred, covered nylon #18 twine from the Wallace Cordage Company. It helps with non-slippage
- Scissors
- Sharp pointed awl
- Tying block: fifteen inches long to wrap twine on and use under your feet to tie corn. (A piece of one inch by two inch wood)
- Knife to splice broom corn stalk and cut
- Five gallon bucket: with water to soak broom corn stalk ends
- Old towel

Trim the tops of the stalks evenly, but leave one half to one inch. Wrap a piece of Velcro around the stalks to keep them down until they dry.

At this point, the broom will be stitched/sewn round for stability. Refer to the instructions for tying a round broom.

Enjoy sweeping those cobwebs away. After sweeping them, wipe with a damp cloth and hang up your broom.

To sew a round broom, you will need twine and a straight sewing needle.

Pull off one yard of twine, tying a knot a one end. Thread the needle with the other end.

Insert the needle through the front of the broom, exiting out the back. Tug on the twine to bury the knot in the middle of the broom.

Wrap the cord clockwise around the broom, passing where you came out in the back and going under the exit point. When you have come to the exit point for the second time, insert the needle below the twine straight through to the other side, coming out above the twine.

Insert the needle below the cord (going over the two cords), pushing to the back of the broom and coming out above the cords.

Insert the needle below the cords angling to one side, splitting front and back, and exiting on top of the cords. Pull snug, causing the loop to indent slightly.

Insert the needle again, going on the bottom of the cords straight across and exiting on the opposite side on top of the twine. Once again give it a slight tug to indent the loop on the other side.

At this point, make a knot onehalf inch away from the broom. When entering the broom at the bottom of the twine, come out anywhere at the top of the broom and pull tightly to bury the knot.

You have now divided your broom into four sections. You may want to complete this task again farther up the broom.

1 Typical cobweb broom handle with a hanger two to three inches from the top and a hole drilled three inches from the bottom for twine.

2 Broomcorn is sorted to use the longer stalks for cobweb brooms.

3 It is good to have your stalks close to the same length to aid plaiting later.

4 Begin placing your broomcorn around your handle to see how many it will take to go around.

5 When you see how many will go around, add a couple just for added measure.

6 Tie the broomcorn and place it in a bucket of water for a minimum of twenty minutes.

7 With twine, tie a double knot to secure it to the handle. Place the soaked broomcorn on a table in front of you, stalks to your left.

8 Wind the twine tightly toward yourself three to four times, stopping in the back.

9 Begin adding broomcorn under the twine one at a time.

10 Add broomcorn side-by-side without overlapping. Pull up on the handle to make a slight dent in the broomcorn stalk after additions.

11 When stalks are added all the way around, wrap three (3) times tightly, stopping in the back.

12 The plaiting will begin one stalk past where the wrap started.

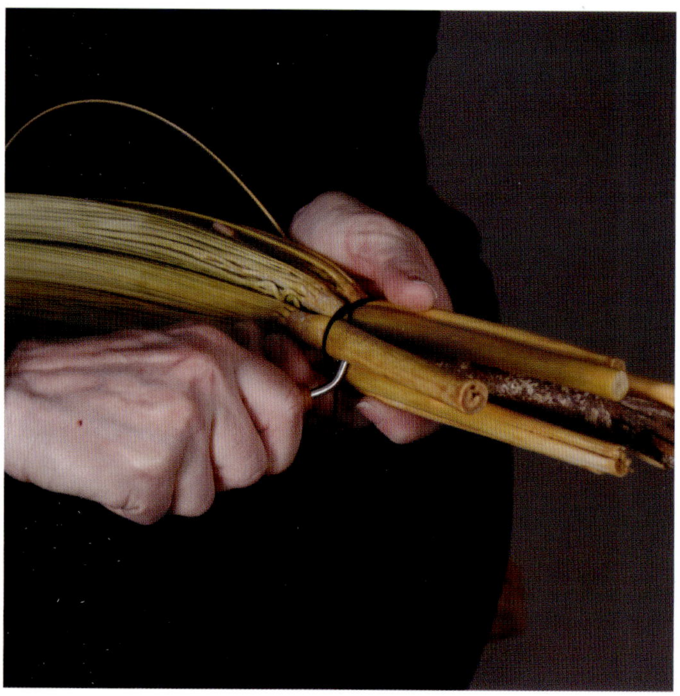

13 At times an awl is helpful to get the twine maneuvered where it needs to be.

14 To plait, weave the twine over-under-over-under-over, continuing around the broom.

15 Ending up with an odd number of stalks is desirable. Splitting one of the larger stalks can aid this being achieved.

16 The split stalk is then woven as two separate ones, thus weaving continuously.

17 The plaiting should start as close to the first three (3) wraps as possible.

18 Pulling the twine toward yourself sometimes aids keeping the weave straighter.

19 Continue the pattern trying to keep the weaving straight; it will naturally spiral on its own.

20 When the plaiting is complete, pace the rip cord under the twining, with the loop end toward the handle.

21 Wrap three (3) times tightly over the rip cord.

22 With your thumb on the wraps, cut the twine and place the end through the loop. Pull the rip cord, thus securing the twine under the wraps.

23 Cut the twine to about an inch.

24 Tuck the tail of the twine under a row of plaiting.

25 Trim the stalks to about an inch. They can be cut shorter when dried.

26 Completed cobweb broom.

27 Double knot with the end short.

28 Place the needle from the front of the broom straight through to the back.

29 Tug slightly to bury the knot in the middle of the broomcorn.

30 Turn the broom clockwise twice, passing under the first twine and stopping in the back.

31 Place the needle under the twine, below where it first came out, straight through to the front.

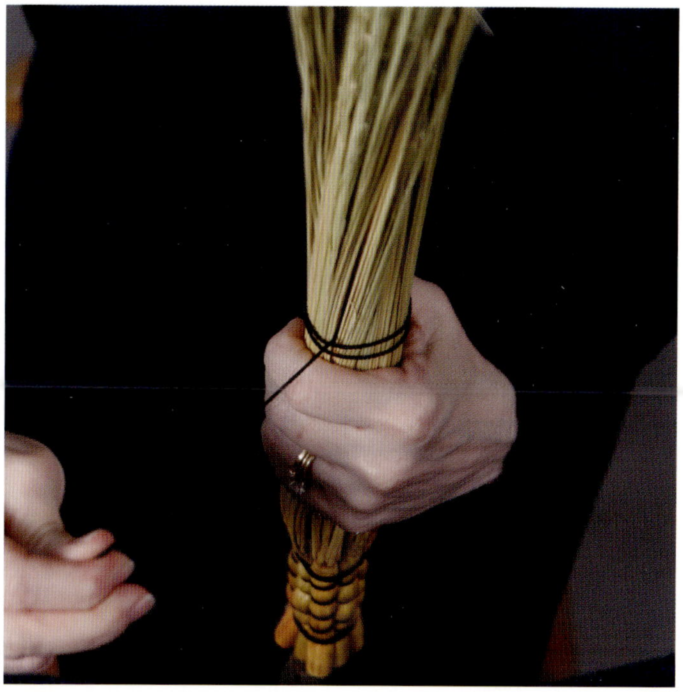

32 Come out in front on top of the twine and pull through.

33 Enter below the twine, going back straight through.

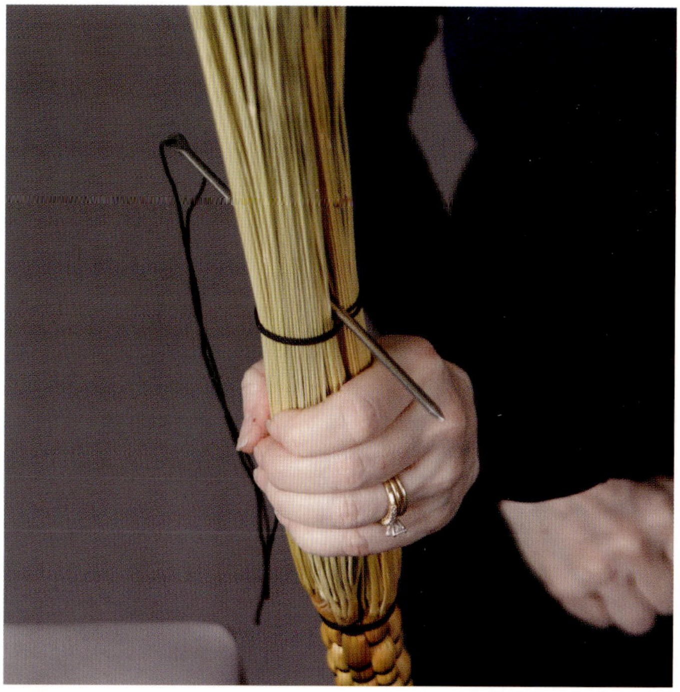

34 Come out above where you first started.

35 Enter below the two twines and go out halfway between the front and back.

36 Coming out on top of the two twines.

37 Enter below and go directly across to the opposite side, coming out on top.

38 Tie a double knot in the twine.

39 The knot should be one inch away from the broom.

40 The needle goes in below the twine, angled up out of the broom on the opposite side.

41 Pull the twine taut, forcing the knot to bury inside the broom. Trim the knot ends.

42 Repeat

Kitchen Broom

INSTRUCTIONS

Finish the handle to where it feels good in your hands. Drill a hole in the tapered end about three inches from the end. Hold the handle against a wall and decide which will be the front and back. I usually sign the back to remind me of my decision. Also drill a hole two to three inches from the top (side to side) to hang with a piece of leather.

Wrap a twine around the tying stick by placing the cord/twine through the hole in the middle and tie a knot—probably two knots. Wrap approximately nine to twelve yards of the cording around the tying stick, not to exceed the three inches in width in the middle. Your feet must have room to hold down each side of the stick on the floor.

Fill your bucket with warm water—enough to cover the stalks of broomcorn, usually about twelve inches. Place your chosen corn in the bucket, stalks down, for twenty to thirty minutes.

Take a piece of your twine (approximately twelve inches), fold in half, and tie together at one end. This is your rip cord at the end of plaiting. Remember to keep it in reach!

When tying on broomcorn, wind toward yourself, handle to your left, palm up, and broomcorn to your right. If left-handed switch hands.

When your broomcorn stalks are getting soft, take out the inner layer bundle and place it on a table.

If doing a double layer or triple layer, the inner layer stalks will be concave. Using a knife, split the stalk in half about a half inch down from the knuckle, then trim all of the split stalks to about three inches; they will not show and will not be plaited.

Tie the twine through the hole at three inches on the handle; tie a good knot. Roll the handle toward yourself—pull—roll—pull—roll—pull (tension taut), stopping in the back. There will always be three wraps stopping in the back. Keep tension tight!

Now start adding the concave broomcorn by placing it *under* the twine, just above the hurl. Continue placing the stalks side by side without overlapping. Wrap three times, keeping tension taught. Now spiral up, wrap three times, and back down the handle to anchor the ends.

Now we will add the shoulders for the broom. Three will be added to each side. The broomcorn will be added in a triangle fashion—two side by side with one on top.

MATERIALS

- **Broomcorn stalks:** enough to go around the handle without overlapping; you will need two layers around the handle. Normally you can measure once around, then take that number of stalks and add three to four more stalks for the next layer. If adding shoulders (three on each side) to the broom, add ten to the third and final layer.
- **Handle:** (3⁄4–1 in.) raw or finished, best if tapered at one end, hole drilled 3⁄16 in. three inches from the end. Your handle before adding broomcorn should be thirty-six to fifty-four inches.
- **Twine:** #18, I use tarred covered nylon; it has tooth and is non-slip. Anything smaller will risk pulling through the broomcorn.
- **Scissors**
- **Sharp pointed or flat awl**
- **Tying block (1 x 2 x 15 1/2 in.):** drill a hole in the middle, wind on to the middle three inches. Feet will be placed on each end to hold your tension. I use these when I travel teach.
- **Knife:** to split broomcorn stalks and cut broomcorn
- **Five gallon bucket:** for soaking broomcorn twenty to forty-five minutes to slightly soften stalks
- **Old towel**

Begin wrapping three times as these three are added to each side. Wrap tightly in the same place where the first row was wrapped.

Now the outer row of the broom will be added. This is the broomcorn that will be plaited up the handle. As with the other layers, bring the broomcorn *under* the twine, just in line with the layer below. The stalks may have to be placed between the stalks of the previous row if you cannot keep them directly on top. When all is added, wrap three times, stopping in the back. Once again, roll—pull—roll—pull—roll—pull, with tight tension.

When the broomcorn is all attached, you will now begin to plait the stalks. Start under the first stalk, just past the center back. Go under, over, under, over, etc. Keep plaiting as close as possible to the twining. After the first row, try to keep plaiting evenly spaced up the handle. The plaiting may be done for a short distance or longer—artist preference.

When plaiting is complete, place the "rip" cord *under* the twine, with the knot end toward the broom end, and wrap three times tightly. Place your non-dominant thumb on the wrap, cut the twine, and place the twine end through the loop of rip cord. Pull the rip cord with your dominant hand, pulling the tail of the twine under the rows of wrap and locking the twine. Cut the end of twine no shorter than one inch. Bury the tail of twine under a row of plaiting using a flat awl.

Trim the tops of the stalks evenly or at a slant, leaving one-half to one inch. Wrap a piece of Velcro, string, or tape around the stalk ends if cut straight across to keep them down until dry. Otherwise they might flare.

1 Handle and two (2) layers of broomcorn.

2 Concave inner layer of the broom.

3 Trim the inner stalks to approximately three inches.

4 Thread twine through the handle; wrap it four to five times around toward yourself.

5 Place broomcorn on the handle half an inch above the knuckle.

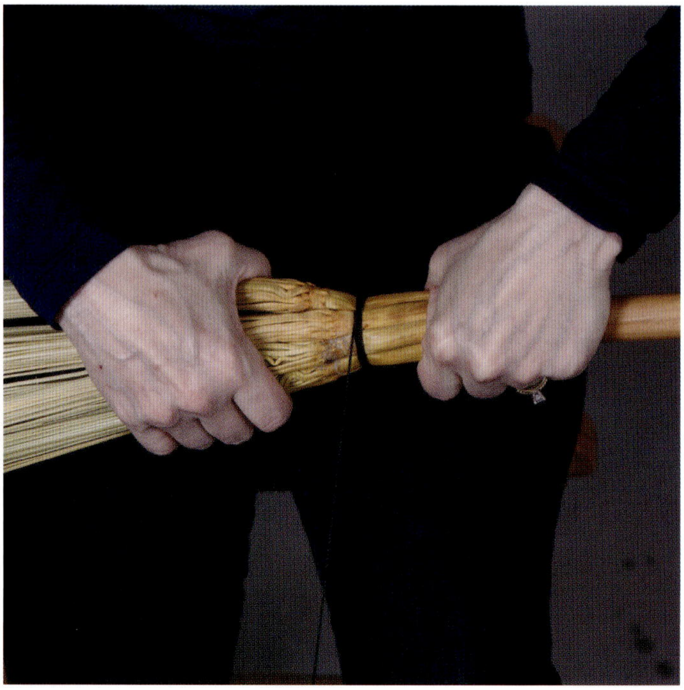

6 After placing broomcorn all the way around, wrap three times.

7 Trim any long inner stalks, then spiral up and back with twine to hold the inner layer down and out of the way of plaiting.

8 Take the outer layer stalks out of the water and keep them within reach.

9 Begin adding the outer layer.

10 Try to keep the twine lined up as you go around.

11 Plaiting begins under-over-under-over, as needed.

12 Try to keep the plaiting straight in the beginning. It will start to spiral naturally.

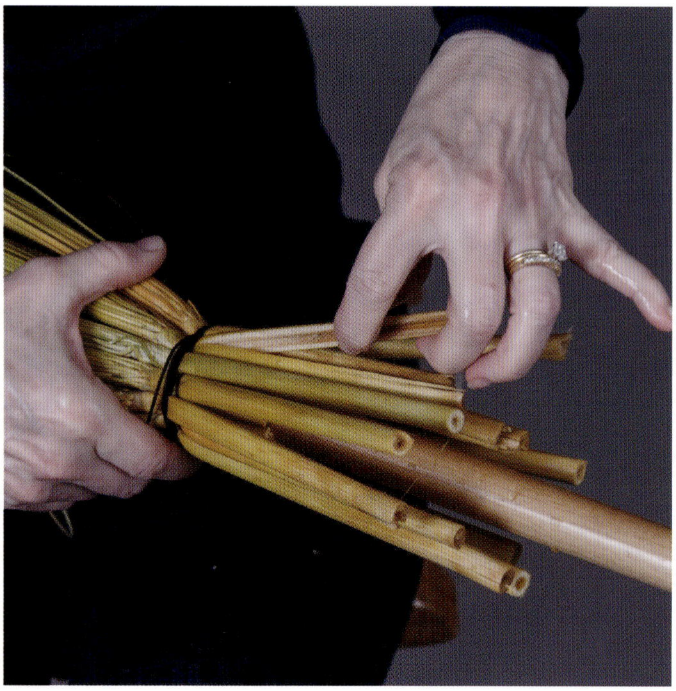

13 It is ideal to have an odd number of stalks. This can be achieved by splitting one of the larger stalks.

14 The split stalk can now be treated as two.

15 Continue plaiting, trying to keep the twine as straight as possible.

16 If a stalk gets crowded out, simply cut off 1 1⁄2 in. and adjust around it.

17 When the plaiting is complete, place the rip cord under the twine.

18 Wrap tightly three times.

19 Placing a thumb on the wraps, cut the twine and place the end through the loop.

20 Pull the rip cord, securing the twine under the wraps.

21 Secure the end under a row of plaiting. Trim the ends of stalks or secure with string and/or Velcro until dry.

Sewing a Flat Broom

INSTRUCTIONS

Thread your needle with two arm/wing spans of cord (approximately 2 1/2 yards). Tie a knot in only one end of your cord.

Place the vise on the broom in such a way that the broom will lay flat against a wall when hung. Make sure the front of your broom is in the front and the back is the back, not to one side. The vise should be close to the plaiting and where you want your first row of sewing.

If using a sewing guide, run it through the broomcorn about one-half to one inch up from the vise toward the sweeping end of the broom.

We will now be referring to numbers on your broom (#1, #2, #3, #4, etc.). Start your needle in the front of the broom in the middle, going through to the back, and coming out at #2 in the back of the broom.

Pull the cordage so the knot is hidden in the center of the broom.

Turn the broom clockwise so that you wrap two turns around. When coming around for the second time stop where you came out, keeping the cordage tight and the broom the width you intend it to be. Insert the needle to the right just past where you came out in the beginning.

When inserting the needle below the cordage in the back of the broom, come out at #1 in the front, above the cordage. Next, insert the needle below the cordage and go across to above the in/out spot and "split the difference." Insert the needle below, "splitting the difference" straight across to the front of the broom and come out above the cordage at the #2 spot.

Again, go in below and come out above at #1 in the back. This now forms a figure eight in the corner of the broom. Some broom makers years ago would say this figure eight must be formed in order for your sewing not to come out. Others would beg to differ. Everyone has their own style and this is just one way.

From this point, you would move down your broom going in below, coming out above, in below, out above, etc., until you have completed the broom across to the other end. When you get to the other side, before entering the broom for the last time, tie a knot in the cordage approximately half an inch from the broom. This time insert the needle across to the middle of the broom and pull the knot into the broom, making sure the knot is hidden inside. Cut the excess off and hide the end in the broom.

If you would like to make two or even three sewn rows across your broom, simply move the vise and continue the same sequence as you did for the first row. After the first row, sometimes it is not necessary to use a vise for the second or third row if your first row has the shape you want for your broom. Some broom makers like the vise to hold on to, or they have a floor vise that holds their broom for them.

MATERIALS

- **Broom needle**
- **Cordage:** Tarred black nylon (my preference)
- **Sewing vise**
- **Sewing guide** (optional)
- **Scissors**

1 Place the broom in a sewing vice.

2 Tighten the vice, ensuring the broom is straight front to back.

3 Insert a needle in through the front middle.

4 Exit the needle in the second position on the back.

5 Gently tug the knot into the middle of the broom.

6 Bring the needle out and wrap the broom to the right twice. Re-enter below where you came out at first.

7 Going straight through to the back, come out on top of the twine and pull through.

8 Take the needle straight back through, under the twine, coming out on top.

9 Go in directly below and angle to the right half an inch.

10 Come out on the opposite side above.

11 Work your way across the broom, paying close attention to spacing.

12 Remove the vice and tie a knot in the twine.

13 Tie a knot close (one half to one inch) above the broom.

14 Bury the knot by running the needle, with knot in twine, through the broom from below the stitches to above somewhere in the middle.

15 You might need to give a little tug to bury the knot.

16 Keep the twine taut while cutting; the knot will pop back into the broom.

17 Repeat if you want a double or triple band.

Hearth Broom

INSTRUCTIONS

As with any handle, it should feel good in your hand. Taper the end and drill a hole three inches up from the end. Hold your handle against a wall and decide which will be the front and back. I usually sign my name to the back to remind me of my decision. Also drill a hole two to three inches from the top (side to side) to thread a piece of leather as a hanger.

Wrap twine around the tying board by placing the cord/twine through the hole in the middle and tie a good knot—probably two knots. Wrap approximately nine to twelve yards of the twine around the board, not to exceed three inches in width in the middle. Your feet must have room on either side to hold the board on the floor.

Fill the bucket with warm water, enough to cover the broomcorn stalks—usually about twelve inches. Place the chosen corn in the water, stalks down, for about twenty minutes or until the stalks are softened.

Take a piece of twine (twelve inches) folded in half and tie the ends together. This is the "rip" cord needed at the end of many tasks. Keep it within reach!

When tying on broomcorn, wind *toward* yourself, handle to your left, palm up, and add broomcorn with your right hand. (For left-handed people just switch hands.)

When your broomcorn stalks are softened, take them out of the water and lay them on a towel on the table in front of you with the stalks to your left.

Tie the twine through the hole at the end of the handle and tie a good double knot. Roll the handle toward yourself pull—roll—pull—roll—pull (tension tight), stopping at the back after three wraps. Wraps in broom making are almost always in threes (some people have their own spin on things to set their brooms apart, with more wraps for decorative purposes).

Start adding broomcorn by bringing the stalks under the twine, just above the knuckle. Continue placing them side by side on the handle, making sure not to overlap.

When all broomcorn is around the handle, wrap three times tightly, stopping in the back.

If doing a double layer, wrap three wraps with the spiral up the concave stalks and back down to start the outer layer. Add the outer layer the same as the previous layer. It sometimes lays better if the additional layer is laid between the stalks of the previous layer. When that layer is on, wrap three times stopping in the back.

MATERIALS

- **Broomcorn stalks:** short, enough to go around the handle without overlapping. If doing a double layer refer to the kitchen broom pattern, except using short stalks.
- **Handle:** 3/4 to 1 in. raw or finished, tapered at one end, with a hole drilled three inches from the end. The handle before adding broomcorn should be twenty-four to thirty-six inches.
- **Twine:** I use a tarred covered nylon twine. It is a non-slip, #18. Anything smaller than #18 has a potential of cutting the broomcorn when pulling tight.
- **Tying Block (1 x 2 x 15 1/2 in.):** hole drilled in the center, wind twine in the center three inches.
- **Scissors**
- **Knife:** to splice broomcorn stalks as needed
- **Five gallon bucket:** to soak broomcorn, stalks down
- **Old towel**

When the broomcorn is attached, begin plaiting the stalks. Start under the first stalk, just past your center back mark. Take the twine under, over, under, over, under, etc. Work in this sequence all the way around until you get back to where you started. *If* you have an *odd number* of stalks you will be able to keep the continual weave. *If* you have an *even number* of stalks, you will need to go over two stalks when you get to the back to reset your sequence (this will make a nice spiral as you come to that same spot each time, going over two). The other option is to split one of the stalks into two stalks, making an odd number of stalks.

Plaiting is the artist's preference. You can only plait as far as your shorted stalk. When plaiting is complete, place the "rip" cord under the twine, next to the last plaiting (toward the broom end with the loop toward the handle). Wrap three times over the rip cord. Place your left thumb on the wraps, cut cord, and place the end of the cord through the loop of the rip cord. With your dominant hand pull the rip cord, thus pulling the cord under the wraps and securing the twine. Cut the end no less than half an inch. Tuck the tail of twine under a row of plaiting using the awl.

Trim the tops of the stalks evenly, or at a slant, leaving one-half to one inch. Wrap with Velcro around the stalk ends if cut straight across to keep them from flaring until dry.

If sewing the Hearth Flat Broom, refer to the Kitchen Broom pattern. If sewing the Hearth Round Broom, refer to the Cobweb Broom pattern.

1 The handle and enough short broomcorn to go around the handle.

2 Wrap the twine around the handle at least three wraps.

3 Broomcorn is added a half inch above the knuckle.

4 Continue adding broomcorn side-by-side without overlaps.

5 When all is added, wrap twine three times around, stopping in the back.

6 Begin plaiting over-under-over-under.

7 Keep plaiting close to the wraps for the first round.

8 Plaiting will naturally start to spread out.

9 An awl can help keep the plaiting tight and uniform.

10 Keep plaiting tight; you should see a slight indent in your weaving.

11 When plaiting is complete, place the rip cord under the twine.

12 Wrap three times, place your thumb on the wrap, and cut the twine. Lace the end through the loop and pull the rip cord, securing the twine under the wraps.

13 Tuck the cut end under a row of plaiting.

14 Trim the stalk ends. Refer to sewing round or flat broom instructions.

Whisk Broom

MATERIALS

- **Broom Hhrl:** enough that your middle finger and thumb nail overlap, approximately one to one and a half inches diameter. (Hurl is broomcorn without the stalk.)
- **Nylon twine:** approximately ten yards
- **7 millimeter flat oval reed** dyed your favorite color: approximately fifteen pieces, six to seven inches long
- **Tying block:** fifteen inches long to wrap twine on and use under your feet to tie corn. (A piece of one by two inch wood.)
- **Basket or pruning shears**
- **Serrated knife or pocket knife**
- **Five gallon bucket:** to soak
- **Old towel**

PLEASE NOTE: Once you start tying this broom, you cannot stop until finished. It is a continuous wrap. Have all tools within reach.

INSTRUCTIONS:

Cut two pieces from the twine: one for the hanger (approximately ten inches) and one for the rip cord (approximately sixteen inches). Fold both in half and tie the loose ends together. Set these aside for later. You could also use leather or other hangers if desired.

Drill a hole in the center of the tying block. Knot the twine through the hole and wrap the twine around it in the center, leaving room for your feet at both ends. Wrap approximately nine to twelve yards of twine around the stick.

Place your 7 millimeter reed in water to soak. Usually thirteen to fifteen will go around your whisk broom handle. It is better to soak too many than not enough. You want an uneven number, unless you are doing a twill plait.

Lay your tying block under your feet so that the twine comes from underneath and next to you.

Take your bundle of hurl and place it in your non-dominant hand, with the soft/wispy ends facing your dominant hand. Slip the twine through the middle of the hurl about four to five inches from the top end of your broom, leaving approximately a two-inch tail. Wrap toward yourself, going around the bundle once, then place the tail of the twine over the wrap and toward your non-dominant hand. Wrap tightly three more times, going up the hurl, over this tail, and toward your non-dominant hand. This catches and locks the end of the twine. This tail will be caught with the other wraps and hidden with the seven millimeter reed covering the top of your whisk broom.

Now holding the broomcorn with your non-dominant hand, "V" up the twine about one-half inch on the side. Continue doing this for as long as you want your handle to be—usually three to four inches—stopping in the back of your broom.

Again, wrap three times toward the wispy end when you get to where you want to stop your handle. Now cross the "V" going the opposite direction going back up the handle to the top.

When you reach the top of your handle, place your handle string and wrap three times, stopping in the back.

At this point you can stop for a break and tie off or continue on. If tying off, place the rip cord with the loop facing the end of the broom. Wrap over this pull string three or four more times. Hold the last wrap with your thumb and cut two to three inches long. Place the end through the pull loop and hold it again with your thumb. With your dominant hand, pull the rip cord, thus pulling the end of the twine under the wraps to secure the end. Cut to approximately one-half inch—*no shorter*! Bury the end down in the hurl of your broom using an awl.

If you choose to continue on, see the instructions for plaiting the tops of whisk brooms. If you stopped, secure a new cord as you started and wrap three more times, stopping in the back, then continue to plait the top.

1 Whisk brooms begin with eight to ten ounces.

2 Bring the twine up through the middle of the bundle.

3 Wrap once, then fold the twine back over to be secured with the next three wraps.

4 Start to spiral 3/8 in. apart.

5 Spiral down toward the sweeping end of the broom for two to three inches.

6 Wrap three times and spiral back.

7 At the top, spiral just above the beginning first wrap.

8 Place the rip cord and wrap tightly three more times.

9 With your thumb on the wraps, cut the twine, place the end in the loop, and pull the rip cord.

10 Trim the twine end and bury it down in the hurl. Refer to previous patterns for plaiting and sewing the broom flat.

Some brooms must be dried prior to sewing flat, or they will mold inside; here brooms are drying in the rafters. *Courtesy of Thompsons Brooms, photo by Karen Hobbs*

Brooms drying in the rafters. *Courtesy of Thompsons Brooms, photo by Karen Hobbs*

Brooms drying. *Courtesy of Sunflower Broom Shop*

Claudie Parson broom with a hand-carved Santa broom handle by Dale DeLong, drying. *Courtesy of Sunflower Broom Shop*

There are two rules of thought on finishes when it comes to any natural material. Some people believe natural materials need to breathe. Therefore, when you apply a polyurethane, oil-based stain, or Deft gloss brushing lacquer to a natural material, it clogs the pores and eventually dries out the broomcorn. Others disagree, stating these materials make their handles and plaiting stronger and last longer. I was taught from a stool caner not to stain natural materials, so I do not get anything on my broomcorn. I ensure handles are sanded really well and are nice to the touch, and at times apply a light coat of clear acrylic to only the handle.

Broom press to hold a broom while sewing. *Courtesy of Broom & Basket Shop, West Amana, Iowa. Photo by Karen Hobbs*

Brooms drying and antique broom press. *Courtesy of Sunflower Broom Shop*

Joanna Schanz sewing a broom using a broom press. *Courtesy of Broom & Basket Shop, West Amana, Iowa. Photo by Karen Hobbs*

CHAPTER TEN

Statistics

Broomcorn Statistics for Various Years 1915–19601

1915	Acreage Harvested 1,000 acres	Yield Per Acre Lb	Production Tons	Price Per Ton Dollars	Value of Production Thous. $$
Illinois	28	480	6,700	$127	$851
Kansas	15	425	3,200	87	278
Oklahoma	240	440	52,800	91	4,805
Texas	6	580	1,700	87	148
Colorado	18	500	4,500	72	324
TOTAL	307	449	68,900	93	6,406
1923					
Illinois	40	510	10,200	$217	2,213
Missouri	1	450	900	171	154
Kansas	70	370	13,000	105	1,365
Oklahoma	273	240	32,800	153	5,018
Texas	51	365	9,300	190	1,767
Colorado	48	365	8,800	138	1,214
New Mexico	50	255	6,400	98	627
1929					
Illinois	21	502	5,300	$162	859
Missouri	1	300	200	94	19
Kansas	50	280	7,000	112	784
Oklahoma	125	287	17,900	119	2,130
Texas	10	294	1,500	116	174
Colorado	64	286	9,200	110	1,012
New Mexico	39	319	6,200	111	688

1944	Acreage Harvested 1000 acres	Yield Per Acre Lb	Production Tons	Price Per Ton Dollars	Value of Production Thous. $$
Illinois	14	600	4,200	$294	1,235
Kansas	22	400	4,400	228	1,003
Oklahoma	109	375	20,400	230	4,692
Texas	43	370	8,000	235	1,880
Colorado	124	350	21,700	200	4,340
New Mexico	70	300	10,500	163	1,712
1960					
Illinois	.4		100	350	35
Kansas	2.7	280	400	300	120
Oklahoma	36	440	7,900	360	2,844
Texas	20	275	2,800	280	784
Colorado	41	240	4,900	315	1,544
New Mexico	37	245	4,500	340	1,530

The broomcorn broom manufacturing industry has been in a slow, long-term decline starting sometime after WWII. The biggest factor was changes in the floor cleaning marketplace. When wall-to-wall carpet cleaned by vacuum cleaners became popular in the 1950s, demand for corn brooms started to decline. Then plastic fiber brooms (starting in the 1960s) started taking some of the remaining market. Also, imported corn brooms made with low cost labor from Mexico started to gain market share. Steep import tariffs limited corn broom imports, but these went away first with the Caribbean Basin Initiative (1983) and finally NAFTA (1994). More recently leaf blowers (1990s) have cut demand for brooms for sweeping decks, patios, driveways, sidewalks, and curbs.

One way broom manufacturers have hurt their market has been by failing to promote quality brooms and instead focusing on making cheap, low quality brooms that are inferior sweeping tools.

PelRay has been importing broomcorn from Mexico since at least the 1940s. Mexican broomcorn did not completely replace American broomcorn until about 1974. This was partially because it became harder to get labor for harvesting broomcorn in the US.

At one time, there were 1,500 broom shops in the US making 45 million brooms. The industry peaked in the late 1920s.

CHAPTER ELEVEN

Broom Lore & Superstitions

- If you hit a person with a broom just before he starts "uptown," he will have trouble before returning.
- Do not sweep immediately after the departure of a guest or you will sweep him bad luck.
- If a broom falls in front of you and you step over it before picking it up, you will have a "bed of sickness."
- If someone comes to see you and you pick up a broom and start sweeping in front of them, that is a sign they are not wanted and you want them to go home.
- To prevent an unwelcome guest from returning, sweep out the room they stayed in immediately after they leave.
- If you hand a broom through a window to somebody you can expect bad luck.
- When you move to a new house, always enter first with a loaf of bread, a new broom, and a bag of salt. You will have good luck and prosperity.
- Never remove an old broom from a house you are moving from. Leave it there. Buy a new broom when you move into your new house. Good luck will follow you and the person who moves into your old house.
- Do not lean a broom against a bed. The evil spirits in the broom will cast a spell on the bed.
- If you sweep trash out the door after dark it will bring a stranger to visit.
- If someone is sweeping the floor and sweeps over your feet you will never get married.
- Sweep under someone's feet and they will be married in a year.
- The pagan harvest ritual of hopping up and down on broomsticks in fields created the imagery for witches flying on broomsticks.
- The broom is a symbol of cleanliness and domestic order.
- A straw broom is always in the corner of a clean house.
- To indicate to your guests they have stayed long enough, simply place a broom on the floor.
- The practice of laying a broom across your threshold on New Year's Day will keep evil spirits away during the remainder of the year.
- The act of sweeping a circle around a mate in any room of the home will keep them eternally true.
- If a single person wishes to get married, he or she should never let anyone sweep a circle around them.
- In the harvest ceremony, brooms were raised up to show how high they would like the crops to grow—if it was all right with the deity.
- A broom dropping in front of a door means company before the day is over.
- For good luck, always pick up a broom that is lying on the floor or ground.
- Always sweep dirt out the back door or you will sweep away your best friend.
- Bad luck will befall you all year if you sweep on New Year's Day.

- If dirt is swept out a door before sunrise you may expect bad luck.
- Carry a broom under your arm for luck.
- If you want your meal to be really good, lay a broom under your dining room table while you are cooking.
- If you want a good night's sleep, put a broom under your bed; it sweeps away all bad dreams.
- If a bride and groom hold hands and jump over a broom, good luck and fortune will abound in their union.
- An old Welsh custom calls for newlyweds to enter their new home by stepping over a broom and luck will follow.
- If you set a broom in the corner, you will surely have strangers come to your house.
- If you sweep on Monday, you sweep your money away.
- It is considered unlucky to lose a mop or broom at sea.
- To drop a broom is a sign of company coming.
- To walk over sweepings is unlucky.
- To loan a broom is a sign of bad luck.
- It is unlucky to carry dirt from one place to another with a broom.
- To rest a broom on the handle behind a door is a sign of thrift.

CHAPTER TWELVE

Broomstick Cake

It is a mystery how this name originated. Perhaps the recipe was envisioned while someone was hungry after exercising. Also, ingredients in the cake (apples, walnuts, and molasses) suggest the fall of the year, when brooms are made.

1. Prepare an 8 x 12 x 2 pan (I use a glass pan) with melted butter (2 tablespoons) and sprinkle brown sugar over the butter evenly.
2. After peeling and coring the apples, cut them into approximately one-half inch thick slices. Arrange the slices over the sugar mixture. Sprinkle with nuts. In a bowl, cream the butter and sugar. Add eggs and molasses, mixing well. Stir the dry ingredients into the creamed mixture until smooth. Add hot water and stir again. The batter will be thin.
3. Pour the batter over the apples. Bake at 350 degrees for thirty-five minutes, or until the cake tests done (with a broomcorn cake tester). Remove from the oven. Loosen the cake around the edges and let stand five minutes before turning out on a serving tray.

Eat only a small piece now if you are watching your weight. Makes eight to ten servings.[1]

INGREDIENTS

1 Egg

3/4 Cup Brown Sugar

2 Tablespoons Melted Butter

5 Medium Cooking Apples

½ Cup Margarine or Butter

2/3 Cup Granulated Sugar

½ Cup Walnuts, chopped

1 Cup Molasses

2 ½ Cups Flour

1 ½ Teaspoons Baking Soda

1 Teaspoon Cinnamon

3/4 Teaspoon Ginger

1/4 Teaspoon Cloves

3/4 Teaspoon Salt

1 Cup Hot Water

Glossary

Angel wing whisk: whisk broom where the broom hurl is added to both sides, thus resembling an angel's dress

Besom: (*bee'-some*) German word for broom

Bract: modified leaf growing on a stalk

Broomcorn: the brush or head used in the manufacture of brooms and brushes

Broomsquire: person who makes brooms for a living

Broom vice: two 1 in. x 2 in. x 15 in. boards with eye bolts and nuts placed together to sew brooms flat

Canaries: Migrant workers, also called "Johnnies"

Fiber: panicle branches extending outward from the knuckle. Sweeping end of the broomcorn

Fireside broom: the fireside or hearth broom originated when the first caveman took a handful of twigs and swept out the old fire pit

Glumes: husks

Handle: the stem

Hurl: a long, fine brush suitable for use on the outside of brooms. Sweeping end of broomcorn without the stalks.

Knuckle: the node where the fibers branch from the stem

Length: short brush (measures less than fourteen inches)

Long: (seventeen to twenty-three inches), or over length (twenty-three inches or over) As determined by measurements of the fiber taken from the knuckle to the top

Medium: (fourteen to seventeen inches)

Panicle: head, spike, or spikelet

Rick curing: broomcorn is spread on racks in a drying shed

Self-working: broomcorn which can be used for the inside and outside of brooms

Tabling: a method of bending tall stalks of broomcorn over, at waist level, diagonally across from adjacent rows, forming a table of crossed stalks with the panicles extending beyond adjacent rows, bringing the head within easy reach of the cutter

Threshing: process of removing seeds from broomcorn

Turkey wing: whisk broom where the hurl is added to one side, thus resembling a turkey's wing. The turkey wing whisk originated in the South during the late 1700s, and was sold as a replacement for the real turkey wings commonly used for sweeping tables, floors, or the hearth

Tying board: 1 in. x 2 in. x 15 1/2 in. board used under one's feet with twine in the middle for tying brooms

Underwork: broomcorn not suitable for hurl

Endnotes

Introduction

1. Leonard W. Labaree, et al., *The Papers of Benjamin Franklin*. New Haven and London: Yale University Press, 1963, Vol. 7, p. 134, 154–5.

Chapter One

1. Marlow Gates, *The Story of the Wedding Broom*. www.friendswoodbrooms.com.
2. Arthur Martin, *The Story of Broomcorn*. Arthur, IL: Rockome Publisher, 1970, p. 3–6.

Chapter Two

1. P. R. Carter, et al., *Broomcorn*. Department of Horticulture, Purdue University, 1990. www.hort.purdue.edu/newcrop/afcm/broomcorn.
2. Bart Pelton, *Care of Your Broom*. National Broom Council Pamphlet.

Chapter Three

1. Ray LeBlanc, PelRay International, LLC., *Harvest to Bale*. PelRay International LLC, Production.
2. Dr. Sam Moyer, PhD, *The Jersey Jerry Broomsquire: Handcrafted Brooms*. Pamphlet, 1977.

Chapter Six

1. Don Rankin, *Broom, Brush & Mop Magazine: 100th Anniversary Centennial Yearbook, 1912–2012*. Arcola, IL: Rankin Publishing, Inc., 2013, p. 136.
2. M. Angeles Villarreal, et. al., *Provisions of North American Free Trade Agreement*. Congressional Research Service, 7-5700, 2015, p. 1, 3–9, 18–20.
3. Bart Pelton, COO of PelRay International, LLC. Interviewed by author March 13, 2014, regarding NAFTA.

Chapter Eight

1. Bart Pelton, *"Sweeping Statements."* National Broom Council Pamphlet.
2. Dr. Sam Moyer, PhD. "Taking Care of Your Broom." *The Jersey Jerry Broomsquire: Handcrafted Brooms*, Pamphlet, 1977.

Chapter Ten

1. Don Rankin, *Broom, Brush & Mop Magazine: 100th Anniversary Centennial Yearbook, 1912–2012*, Statistics Archives. Arcola, IL;:Rankin Publishing, Inc., 1915–1960.

Chapter Twelve

1. Alice Babbs Smith, *Broomcorn Nostalgia: Field of Memories*. Santa Barbara, CA: Old Mill Publishing, 1996, p. 182.

Bibliography

Carter, P. R., *et al. Broomcorn*. Department of Horticulture, Purdue University, 1990.

Gates, Marlow. *"Jumping the Broom"* www.friendswoodbrooms.com (wedding brooms).

Labaree, Leonard. *The Papers of Benjamin Franklin*. New Haven and London: Yale University Press, 1963, Vol. 7, p. 134, 154–5.

LeBlanc, Ray. *Harvest to Bale*. PelRay International, LLC, Production.

Martin, Arthur. *The Story of Broomcorn*. Arthur, IL: Rockome Publishing, 1970.

Moyer, Sam, PhD. *The Jersey Jerry Broomsquire: Handcrafted Brooms*. Pamphlet, 1977.

National Broom Council. *A Clean Sweep for Ben's Brooms*. Chicago, Illinois.

Pelton, Bart. COO, PelRay International, LLC, in discussion with the author, July 2014.

Rankin, Don. *Broom, Brush & Mop Magazine: 100th Anniversary Centennial Yearbook, 1912–2012*. Arcola, IL: Rankin Publishing, Inc., 2013.

Smith, Alice Babbs. *Broomcorn Nostalgia: Field of Memories*. Santa Barbara, CA: Old Mill Publishing, 1996.

Villarreal, M. Angeles, et. al., *Provisions of North American Free Trade Agreement*. Congressional Research Service, 7-5700, 2015, p. 1, 3–9, 18–20.

Contacts

The following contacts have supplies and classes:

Maggie Lane Studio,
www.maggielanestudio.com

PelRay International, LLC.,
210-757-4640, www.PelRay.com

Caddy Supply Company,
803-829-7072, www.caddysupply.com

Royalwood, Ltd.,
800-526-1630, www.royalwoodltd.com

John Campbell Folk School,
800-365-5724, www.folkschool.org

Leese & Wayne Thompson,
256-446-5555, www.thompsonsbrooms.com

Wallace Cordage Co.,
800-743-7475, www.wallacecordage.com

Acknowledgments

I would like to dedicate this book to all of my students who have taken my broom classes, keep coming back for more, and challenge me to come up with new broom designs. Keep up the great work and keep sweeping those cobwebs!

And to my wonderful husband, who has encouraged me through this journey to write a book, taking me to places I would have never dreamed of going so that I could work with and observe other broom makers. Thank you for building me a great studio where I can leave my mess and you never say a word. You cook for me and take loving care of me through my health issues. You are the most caring, patient, and loving man I have ever known; I love you Cisco.

Every effort has been made to ensure that the information in this book is accurate, but in different parts of the US and the world people learn differently.

I want to thank those who helped me along the way to make this book become a reality:

Flo Hoppe, for all of the encouragement and advice about writing a book, and sharing all the ups and downs that come with doing so. Also for the friendship over the years and always being a joy to be around.

Ben and Becky Rehder, for sharing a wealth of information about writing a book and for your first lessons learned.

Anne Jordan, for her expertise in helping me understand contracts and being more comfortable with them. A patient and loving sister-in-law—thank you.

Bart Pelton, you opened up not only your business, but your family history to me. You welcomed me into your conference room and allowed me to spread out books and precious memories of family photos, sharing wonderful stories about the broomcorn industry for the past one hundred plus years. You were always there to answer my many questions.

Ray LeBlanc, for the many stories about the broomcorn business past and present. You entertained many of my questions about the industry.

Helen Cannon, for teaching me how to make my first broom at John Campbell Folk School.

Pat Monahan, it was great being in Arcola, Illinois during the Broomcorn Festival and seeing firsthand how the whole town participates in the festivities. You shared a lot of information about the history of the "Broomcorn Capital of the World" and the Lawn Rangers. Fun was had by all participating in the parade.

Leesa and Wayne Thompson, for sharing all aspects of broom making and dying hurl. You taught me alternative ways to tie brooms and how to use a kick wheel. Wayne, your knowledge of broom making and broom making equipment is endless.

Diane Wilson, for organizing, typing patterns, and making sense of them all.

Sherry Muehlfarth, for being a loving sister through my treatments and all the encouragement and edits while writing this book.

Zachary Alan Photography, my photographer for pattern photography.